Who Am I Not to Shine?

Owning Your Purpose
As the Leading Lady
You Were Created to Be

Christina Johnson

Who Am I Not to Shine?
Owning Your Purpose
As the Leading Lady
You Were Created to Be
Christina Johnson

Dedication

I dedicate this book to my daughters Ariana and Isabella. I am blessed that God gifted me with such intelligent, determined, creative, and beautiful girls. I love your cheerfulness, questions, and opinions. You girls inspire me! May you continue to do your best, pursue your dreams, keep God first, and receive every good thing you desire. Mommy loves you!

Acknowledgements

I first want to give thanks to God, my Director and Producer for giving me the vision and words to complete this book and keeping me daily. For being so supportive and listening to all of my ideas, no matter what time of day or night, a huge thank you goes to my husband, Glen Watkis. Thank you for believing in me and being there when I wanted to stop and for providing me the space, time, and finances, as I focused on this project. I love you! To my wonderful daughters, thank you for being patient and understanding during the times I had to give my attention to writing. This is for you! Even the sky isn't a limit for you two. You girl's rock!

For your leadership, your resiliency, your support, and writing the forward for this project, many thanks goes to you, Althea Webber-Bates! I love and appreciate you sis and I am glad that our paths crossed. Sistah Nandi, I am grateful that you are a part of my network. I remember being a child in Sankofa Kuumba dance program and witnessing your strength and drive for community. Then as two adults we met again, you not knowing me, but me remembering you, and we both felt a connection. God works in mysterious ways. Because of you, I am taking the word try out of my vocabulary, because you told me not to try, and *just do*. We spoke on the phone one night about a project and you didn't know it, but I was thinking about giving up on an idea and you gave me words of encouragement and told me not to settle. It was right on time, so thank you! Forever my Mama C! Sistah Nandi, I love you!

Getting this project complete was fun and rewarding. And for the cover, I could not have done it alone; it was truly a team project. Sure it was my vision, but it would not have come to life visually without a team. To my talented photographer, Tepheret Jones, thank you for capturing the vision just right! I love your energy and spirit. Not to mention, you do wonders with that camera and editing equipment! AMJ Photography is on the rise and I can't wait to see where you take it. Sasha Thompson of

ArgentineRose, thank you for taking time out of your busy schedule to decorate my face! You also helped to give me a reminder lesson on entrepreneurship, communication, and forgiveness that will stay with me. I thank you both for being a part of this project! I give to you my gratitude and I look forward to what's to come.

To my earthly father, Curtis Johnson, thank you for all of your encouraging words, help, and prayers. For our talks, Missy-Lynn Lewis-Thank You! You are and always have been my sounding board. I am so grateful to have you in my life. We were born as cousins, but you are truly my best friend. Thank you for being there! Salonika, you are an inspiration and you have grown into such a responsible young woman. I am super proud of you! Stay positive. I love you! Malachi, young King and comedian, you can do anything you put your mind to. Know that. I love you! To my sister, Kamirre, thank you for looking out for me. You came through when I didn't have it. Your strength and advice reminded me of my accomplishments when I forgot what I was capable of. I love and appreciate you! Aunt Stephanie, thank you for taking me in as your own and raising me. Your encouragement and example helped me to be the woman I am today. You really did earn that Diploma, lol (Insider). Thank You! Your positivity and faith are inspiring. Aunt Velma, thank you for always checking in on us, it means a lot. Aunt Velma and Uncle Joel, thank you for spending time with the girls. It gives me a much-needed recharge and they enjoy their time. I sure appreciate you guys! Uncle Van, a piece of this book was inspired by some of those hard and trying times we discussed. I thank you for your guidance and for your support at a few points when I was going through. To my long time mentor and big brother Trevor Foster, thank you for being one that tells it like it is. I may not have always liked the things you say, but you speak your truth. Thank you for being an example, for encouraging me, and believing in me. Anyone that has given me an encouraging word in person, through social media, or otherwise you are greatly appreciated. May we continue to pass the torch! To God be the glory!

6

CONTENTS

FORWARD

Althea Webber Bates
*Consultant, Women/Girls Expert, Author, Resiliency Coach,
Motivational Speaker/Trainer*

Hi Life Directors and Producers,

Welcome to this journey to help you discover you and shine
in the process. I am so excited that you have decided to take
this journey to learn, grow and define your best you. I am so
honored to have the opportunity to learn and grow from my
own life experiences and share some of the tools, tips, and
strategies I picked up along the way with you. Life is truly the
teacher of many of our lessons and the tester of those same
lessons as well. I love the me I have discovered and the me I
currently am. I worked hard for her through my own self-
discovery process. It took me a while to find my own inner
leading lady in my actual story and not the story I told
myself. She was a hidden gem, a prize, a diamond in the
rough and a rose like none other, but didn't know it.

I would like you to consider this book *Who Am I Not to Shine*
as the manuscript to your own life! What role do you want to
play in your own story? For myself I spent much of life
allowing fear to dictate what happened in my own story.
Growing up I was super shy and quiet and elected many
times not to speak unless I had to. I spent most of my life
observing the people, places and things around me. I also
spent much time wishing and hoping that I had a completely
different outgoing personality that would allow me be more
confident, have high self-esteem, be bold and be more of a
risk taker. Truly this was not the case in my own life as I
chose to be the understudy to my own main character. I
allowed fear to paralyze me. How about you? Has fear, lack of
self-esteem, or lack of confidence ever prevented you from

being resilient and taking charge over your life? Well Christina Johnson has created a manuscript in *Who Am I Not to Shine* that I wish my younger self had available to assist in moving me into the lifestyle I desired sooner. Many times, we feel that we are alone in the ups and downs, twists and turns life takes us on. Through self-discovery in learning how to become the leading lady in directing your own story you, will discover ingredients to your secret sauce.

What would you say is in your own secret sauce? We all have something special that makes us unique individuals. We all have our own recipes with special ingredients. The question is: How do you tap into the creation of your very own secret sauce?
Well this requires a deeper look at each of our own ingredients and looking at what purpose it serves in our lives. What does our secret sauce taste like? What does our secret sauce look like? What does our secret sauce smell like? What ingredients do you need to add to your secret sauce to make it more potent or more robust? Are we willing to remove ingredients that take away from the taste and smell of our sauce? The discovery of your secret sauce will not only change how you view yourself, but what you allow yourself to be emanated to the outside world. Take the time to engage actively in using this book as a tool and vehicle for discovery to find these hidden ingredients in your secret sauce.

I have had the pleasure of collaborating with Christina Johnson the Author of this wonderful book in hosting women empowerment events and activities and can testify to her passion, purpose and devotion related to young girls and women. We share very similar principles, values and visions for supporting young girls and women who are in need of finding a path to their own vision and purpose.

As a Consultant, Author, Resiliency Coach, Motivational Speaker/Trainer and thought leader in the area of girls and women I understand the varying areas of personal development that many struggle with including fear, lack of confidence, lack of self-esteem etc. One thing that I have come to understand in the work I do, especially with women and young girls is that we are all linked to one another and our connection to one another brings forth healing, growth, and resiliency. I would not only encourage you to take this guided journey of self-discovery, but I challenge you to invite someone else in your inner circle to take it with you. In doing so, you become accountable to someone else in committing to your exploration and self-discovery to bring its manifestation. The chapters outlined in this manuscript for your life from Chapter 1 Co-Producing Your Smash Hit to Chapter 15 The Premiere allow you the space and permission necessary to explore the you that you know you could always be.

Stop perpetuating reasons and excuses not to be great. You have the tools and power already within you to withstand anything that you would encounter as impediment in your path to greatness. Even if the stumbling block in your path to greatness is you.

Imagine your role, don't be afraid to write or re-write your story and produce it as well as co-direct your own life production starring you!

Counting on your success,

Althea Webber Bates
CEO and Founder of Project Resiliency Movement, LLC and A. Bates Consulting Group, LLC
Consultant, Women/Girls Expert, Author, Resiliency Coach, Motivational Speaker/Trainer
Author of Destination Resiliency: A Self-care Planner and Guide and Brokeness, Baggage and Blessings
Co-Author of Life Balance for the Women on the Rise
Co-Author of Soaring Into Greatness
www.abatesconsultingroup.org

INTRODUCTION

Hey Brilliant Beauty!

Yes, I am talking to you and I am glad that you decided to read this book! I hope that you are feeling great today! If not, perk up because you are amazing! I am so excited for you! You are embarking on a journey of self-love, reflection, and growth. You were created to do incredible things and to live a wonderful life. It takes work on your part though. You have to play your role and take full control of the Co-Director's chair. This book is full of information, stories of my personal experiences, tips, advice, and questions to analyze your own life. Think of it as a tool to help you gain perspective on your purpose, faith, relationships, and your role as a lady in this world. Commitment to developing yourself yearly, daily, and hourly is necessary. As long as you have breath you have another chance at anything, just don't give up!

I just love a good movie filled with love, humor, drama, and an empowering ending! How about you? What is your favorite movie and why? Chances are the movie evokes some type of emotion out of you. It is full of ups and downs, twists and turns, but at the end of each situation, the characters usually come out on top or at least okay. This sure does mirror life, hence this book title and theme.

When you look at your own life as a movie and realize that you are Co-Director, you can see that you have a lot to do with controlling your own destiny. You are not able to control other people or all situations, but you can always control your responses and decision-making. This is what gives you power. And because you think and are made different than every other human being, this is what makes you a powerhouse. No one can fulfill your purpose the way you can. How I see it is, good things happen and bad things happen, and we can learn from both. Positive things are great. And the best way to deal with life when negative things happen is to turn them into positive things.

So, are you ready to take "Action" in your life? Or are you at a point where you need to scream "Cut!" as you breathe, pause, and re-evaluate? Both are actually cool and great stepping-stones. It is your movie darling, so let's do what you believe is necessary. If you are ready for action, it's time to plan the direction, keep the momentum and go for it boldly. On the other hand, if you are in need of a break or are feeling lost, you are at a great point to start over and level up. Remember, if someone or something does not fit the life you dream, it is ok to let go.

Inspiration for this book first came while looking at my young daughters so innocently smiling, playing, and dancing in our home. I sat there wishing the best for them and their futures. Really wishing I could keep them away from all mistakes and anyone that could cause them even a tidbit of harm. Then I remembered that although I birthed them and am doing the best I can at raising them, I know that they are only a gift to me and placed on this earth for a specific purpose so I can't shield them from everything. Like mine, their pain will be a part of their purpose.

I thought about the trials and tribulations that I've been through on my journey and how I wanted different for them. Better for them. That's when I wondered how our relationships would be when they get older and of those interesting conversations we will someday have. Then after spending time and talking with my niece, and hearing of how some of the teenagers behave, I realized, real help and guidance is needed. There is so much information I want to share with them, which is why I chose to write a manual that I would like to share with my daughters, niece, and all the daughters of the world.

Wanting to be my daughter's number one most positive role model, I also had to take a good look at myself, and what I had to pass on to these young impressionable children. If not me, they will find someone, the media, a friend, another relative, or possibly a person that may not be beneficial to their lives, to follow. So I realized I had to get it together and put what I've learned to use and show them what a real woman can do, can be, and how they can reinvent themselves daily. I want them to know that as woman of integrity, we don't have to cheat, lie, put others down, or sleep our way to get farther in life. I would like them to lead and not follow, to be independent, to be happy, to love themselves, to choose healthy relationships, be self-sufficient, and to know themselves as God's children.

Young lady, as you make your way through your life journey, make the decision to choose joy and happiness everyday. You will make many mistakes along the way, but they are necessary for your growth. Take failures as learned lessons to share, evolve, and know that through all obstacles put in your way, you can do anything! No matter what! That is your true power! You are a gift here placed for a purpose. God doesn't make mistakes, so it's no coincidence that you are here right now, that you look the way you do, believe what you do, and that you have the talents you do. Your Producer and Executive Director (God) created you for a time such as this. It is time to work toward building the life you want because you are the leading character and Co-Director in this movie called, Your Life.

Miracles & Blessings,

Christina Johnson
     A.K.A.
Classy Chrisy

Chapter 1
Co-Producing Your Smash Hit

Chapter 1
Co-Producing Your Smash Hit

This book could have been released years ago, like in 2010. That is when I began to write it. I had just had my first daughter and I wanted to create a manual from mom that could guide her through life. So why didn't I complete it then? I'd like to say that I was just too busy or life got in the way, but the truth is I was afraid. I was not ready. My confidence was jacked up because I knew I wasn't perfect and did not have it all together. I felt unqualified to teach others. I still have the fear at times, but my goal to teach my girls about life, what to avoid, how to accept themselves, and not let the media taint their self-image, now outweighs that fear. Not long ago, I finally thought, 'if I am really going to believe that I was designed in His image then I sure am going to live like it'. It was God who gave me these words and ideas. And God gave me the gift and ability to put it into writing. And it was sure enough God who made it so that I would be a mother so I did not have a choice, but to teach in order to do my best in this role. So who am I to decide what is not for me?

I have been reconnecting with my Creator and He is leading me on an amazing path. I had to say no to insecurity, no to lack, and no to fear. I even had to say good-bye to hurt and anger. It is not that these feelings don't creep up, it's just that I do my best not to let them rule, the way I used to. As the Creator and Producer of *My Life*, I asked God to take away the desire for anything outside of His will and open up the doors to the things He wants for me. I believe that He answers this prayer daily. Opportunities are coming, ideas are flowing, and a few people and things I had are going. I am the Director of my life and I'm qualified to do anything that I dream. With God as my Producer, who's going to stop me?! You have that same ability. If you have an idea that eats at you and won't let you go, I dare you to go after it! Pursue that thing with God and you will make it!

Even if I have to go forth trembling, I am now going for every goal I want to accomplish. I no longer want to dream of better and wish for change, when I can make it happen. This movie may have been a best-kept secret, but the jig is up. I may have felt broken, insecure, afraid, and weak at times, but I am still energetic, confident, strong, creative and brave. It's my movie and I'm getting ready to release it! You better claim your spot on the chart!

New movies are being made every day. Some low budget, going straight to DVD and others are Number One Blockbuster hits on the big screen. Although they have different levels of budget and screen size they all come from a creative space and a place of intention. The Producers and Directors knew exactly what the outcome was and how it should appear. That is how we should be looking at our lives. What do we want the end product to look like? How would we like to impact others? What is it that we want to do daily?

If you know exactly what career you want to be in, how you want to make impact, and how to get there, that is awesome! But for many of us it is trial and error, leaping, making mistakes, learning, growing, and trying again. To get closer to your purpose ask yourself these questions, What have you always loved to do? What are you naturally good at? What types of things have you always disliked? I want you to think about the answers throughout life so that you can stay focused on your purpose. The answers are clues to your future! Next, go gain some experience in the field to find out whether you really like the career or not. It's a shame how much time and money is wasted on dreams and degrees people think they want to realize it's not really their thing or it doesn't make them happy. The frustration comes from lack of real life exposure. I know that if I was connected to what I was really passionate about at an earlier age I'd be even further in my career now. I am grateful for the journey though, because I am sure I learned some necessary information along the way. I accept that time is also crucial and maybe I needed to learn a few lessons first, so I don't regret it.

I had a journal ever since I can remember and as soon as I would finish one, I would go to the next. I had a lot to write about. Writing is therapeutic, and little did I know growing up, but one title I was meant to have is *Author*. These were clues, but people around me did not know how to guide me here. My Aunt Stephanie told me I did not have a choice, I was going to college, lol. I'm happy I did. So she helped. I love her for that and so much more! My Aunt Velma encouraged my writing and told me she thought that Journalism would be good for me. So she helped guide me toward the path in a way as well. I went to the University of Hartford and began with a major in Journalism. I decided to graduate with a BA in Mass Media Communications, after learning about other creative areas in the field. I never had a job past intern in this field, but what I did not know then is that all of the knowledge would be used in my business and marketing endeavors.

Another thing I loved to do growing up was making paper dolls. My cousin and best friend Missy and I would make paper dolls, clothes for them, food, pets, toys, cars, you name it. We had a field day! And we had Barbie dolls, plenty of them! We just chose these and created what we liked with no limits. I had a few relatives say to me as an adult that they thought we would be Fashion Designers, I just wished I had that information sooner. I honestly did not realize that Fashion Design was a career. Like, I knew people made clothes, but as a career?... I just never thought of it. It would have been awesome if I had that seed planted by those around me. I really enjoy making up a nice story line and I love fashion. Not trendy fashion, but classy, real lady-like and gentleman fashion. That is my thing! I am a Creator and Visionary, I have an abundant amount of ideas, some of which I can't wait to soon share with the world! All of these things were clues to my future, which is my current, present, and some future endeavors.

In writing this book, my goal is to help my daughters and other young women to figure out and decide what your path is sooner than later. What type of movie do you want to Produce? You can choose anything and even mix genres. Do you want a romance? A comedy? A Thriller? Sci-Fi? Most people don't want a horror film, but you will have some crazy periods in life that will feel horrific, so we will go into coping with that as well. Your goal just has to be to stay on purpose. Focus on your goal through good and bad. Take the time to breathe, rest, grieve, forgive, and process information as needed, but don't stay there. The Earth keeps spinning and time keeps moving so you must keep going as well. Being alive is a gift, so bless the world with your presence.

You may want to own a home, get a fancy car, have your dream career, start a business, have happy relationships, you may want children, and/or to vacation often. Whatever your dreams and goals are, you can reach them. If you desire it, that means it is in reach. You would not have the desire if it were not meant for you. Many people give up due to frustration, feeling that they are unable to reach their goals. Sometimes the finances, the network, the support, the job offers, and more are just not visible. We don't see how, so we convince ourselves that what we have is enough. You may even feel guilty at times for not being content and just appreciating what you have already been blessed with. Well let me tell you something that not everyone will. It is okay not to be content with the status quo. This is not to say don't be thankful, because you should be grateful for life and all you have every day. It is completely ok to want more out of life. Some people will be completely satisfied with what you have right now, but that is for them. There is more in store for you if that is what you desire!

You have the best Director in the world and galaxy in your corner to help you produce the life you desire. That Director is God, the ultimate Creator. Your drive and your God are the keys to get you there. He will protect you and guide you. He has your best interest at all times and He placed you here for a purpose even bigger than yourself. What gifts, talents, and ideas did He give you? It is time to use them. It does not matter how old or young you are, there are too many ways to get yourself out there once you just decide to say yes.

Your feature film is going to be bananas! In the most awesome way! Take the time to think and reflect, then answer these questions honestly and openly.

1. What have you always loved to do?

2. What are you naturally good at?

3. What types of things have you always disliked?

4. What do people ask for your help or opinions with? Others can some times see things we don't, so pay attention to the patterns.

5. If you could do anything in the world and know that you would not fail, what would that be?

Chapter 2
The Casting Call

Chapter 2
The Casting Call

I can imagine that finding the leading character is the easiest and toughest part of finding the perfect cast. The Producer must know their vision for what this person will look like, sound like, and how they will behave. Envisioning this person's look and personality may come easy, but finding the perfect individual can be a task. Before we get too deep into casting for your film, go take a look in the mirror. Yeah right now! The beauty you just saw is the leading lady of your feature film. Say, "I love you!" She is so perfect for this role! Tell her "You got this!" Be sure that she has what she needs and give her the star treatment. Everyone else has to flow around you as the main character. Sure there will be times when you have to work with people you don't agree with. There will even be relatives, classmates, and co-workers that you don't care for, but you have to be around, so learning to adjust and knowing where to place people is critical.

What you can choose, is who has major roles versus those who will be just extras. So you have to look at who really fits the script for your big feature film and distance the rest. This is the only time during a casting call when you want to cut the good actors. Like get rid of them completely. We don't have time for fake people, friend, family, or foe. That statement *keep your friends close and your enemies' even closer* is crazy to me. I get that we may like to know what our enemies are plotting against us, but I just can't live this way. So I won't attempt to teach this to you. Cut bad relationships and let them deal with heir own karma. If you have God on your side, He will fight the battles for you. "No weapon formed against you shall prosper." Isaiah 54:17. And just to be certain, He never said the issues and the attacks wouldn't come, He said they would not prosper. So know that you got this because He has full control. After all, the fight's not fair when you have God taking up for you.

Are you ready for a romantic relationship? Are you currently in a relationship? They can be great if they are a good fit and both people are ready, willing and mature enough to handle a real commitment. On the other hand when a relationship is wrong, it is wrong. And it can cause you to feel all out of whack. Try putting two people in a box together, one is an individual that speaks Mandarin only and the other speaks French only and keep them there for a few days and see what type of disaster that will turn into. That's what a relationship between a male and female can feel like during the rough times. I swear for goodness! Those guys speak Shabok and if you speak English like me, you won't always get what they're saying, nor know what the heck Shabok is. They won't always get you either. You just want to find someone who is willing to work through the tough issues.

Seriously though, romantic relationships are full time jobs of their own, and can take a lot of emotional energy. An unhealthy relationship can derail you and take your whole movie off the set. An unhealthy relationship had me feeling like I was losing my mind, caused me to feel insecure, and lose self-esteem. There are dudes who will tell you they love you, have sex with you, and maybe even buy you things, but are telling another female the same things! They may go as far as having another phone to hide it. This is all while you are giving your all and really in love. Ouch! Talk about pain. I've actually been there, so I know. And it does not matter how much you do for them or how you look. Some people are who they are and are going to do what they want to do. This is related to their own personal flaws and usually a shortcoming on their end. So take it personal enough to part ways, but not enough to let it destroy the beauty of you. Giving chance after chance and trying to look past it only prolongs the hurt and only opens the door to more betrayal. I love that Maya Angelou said, "When people show you who they are believe them." Now whether they have mistreated you before or something just doesn't feel right, trust it. That is your inner spirit, and it *knows*.

Life and experiences will give you hints that your intuition will pick up on, so if you are thinking cheater, liar, abuser, woman-beater, womanizer, dead beat, killer, molester, or anything else, listen, pray, obey, and walk away! Experiencing any of these is so not what I wish for you. You deserve to be loved, respected, cared for, checked on, and pampered. You deserve affection, gifts, gentleness, thoughtfulness, and to be told the truth. The script may not be a good fit for them, but don't forget that your script and vision are *perfect for you*!

Anyone that tells you that you require too much just does not deserve a role in your film. Be sure that you are whole yourself before entering into a relationship with another person so that you are not trying to validate yourself through them. Don't give anyone that role, but your maker, God Himself. Be happy with you because you were fly before them and will be fly without them. You were born to soar! They had no parts in that! If you choose your mate wisely and select the right willing person, then both of you should be equally working hard at it together and you both can create happy experiences.

Stick to your word and expect the same. Have standards and expectations of what you want in a mate and don't settle for just anybody. It is important to find someone who compliments you, where you are weak they are strong and vice versa. Couples should have the ability to pick the other up when they are down, I don't mean physically. When one is sad or worried the other should show care, be stable, and be able to make sound decisions. And know that you may marry your high school sweetheart, but be ok if that is not the case. You grow so much in your 20's and 30's that neither of you may be the same person 5-10 years from now. You are still learning your likes, dislikes, and what you really want in a relationship.

If a relationship does not work out and pass on to the next round of casting, do yourself a favor and move forward. Don't sit around wondering if you will ever fill that role. You will. You may wonder whether or not they will finally get their life together or if they will treat the next person better than they did you. There are only two answers and neither changes your relationship with the person. 1- They will treat them better due to growth, lessons learned, and what was meant to be, or 2- They will treat the person the same or worse because something in them is just not right, their selfish, immature, and just not relationship material. I write this remembering my thoughts when I went through break ups or wanted to end relationships, but was afraid. So I have experience here, so I get it and it's not easy. You are not alone if you ever had these thoughts. It's just that these thoughts limit us, telling us that there are not enough options and maybe we are not enough. Well news flash! You are enough! You will have that awesome relationship you desire some day and it will satisfy all of your physical and emotional needs.

What about your friends? I have always loved that song by TLC. How about you? It's such an oldie, but goodie. But really, let's talk about your friends. First I want to let you know that all you need is one or two good friends in life, don't get caught up in wanting to have a bunch of friends, unless you choose to. The younger you are the flakier people may be and as you get older bonds get tighter. You may also learn more about each other as you grow and choose to part ways. Just know that that friendship will be replaced. The people I call friends are open to communication from me and they know that I am open to their honesty. We are there for each other during tough times and good times as much as we can. These friends don't force me to be someone I am not and I accept them for themselves. When I was a teenager I had friends who liked to drink and smoke. It wasn't my thing, although I tried it out of choice. I didn't judge them for doing so and they did not judge me for choosing not to. I want the same for you. If you find yourself around people who try to encourage, force, or say that you are not cool because you choose not to indulge in brain altering activities, find new friends. That's called peer pressure. Try not to fall into that. Decide to be and set your mind on being a leader. You have places to go and it does not include being out of your mind. Let them know this and wear your belief as a badge of honor. It is an honor to be friends with someone like you, so they are privileged to have the chance to hang out with you.

Sidebar: Stay away from bullies, stand up to bullies, and do not become a bully. A bully is someone who uses power, position, or strength to harm, intimidate, or influence someone else. Yes being a leader and influencer can be good, but only when we leave others with choice. We want people to follow, compliment, and imitate us because they choose to. At least I do. I want to have a positive impact that lasts and is a guide for others. This brings me to negative relationships or associates and peer pressure. Don't ever feel as though you must drink alcohol to have fun. Also, no matter who's doing it, don't engage in smoking cigarettes, weed (marijuana), ecstasy, and I pray you never attempt dust, crack, cocaine, or heroine. These are all hard to kick and they cause major damage to your body and brain. I love my body and my brain. How about you? If that's what they use for fun, find new friends and/or associates. You have no time to get caught up in any of the things listed in this paragraph or any new drug or fad that you may hear of. No matter how cool it sounds or looks. Say no to drugs! Say no, be it using them or selling them. Both can easily lead to jail, sickness, and death. That's not for you boo! Our purpose is greater than that!

Be happy letting people go if they are causing you pain. This goes for partnerships, people you thought were friends, as well as some family members. There are some friendships that I have had since elementary school. Others I met and there was an instant bond that keeps us connected even though we don't talk every day, but we are still very close.

And there are some people I met through the years and thought that we would be friends forever and it did not turn out to be the case. Some of these people hurt me, some I may have hurt, and others we just grew apart with our own busy lives. I've learned to be okay with all of this and you will have to adjust as well.

With this, you must discover who the villains are in your life so that you know where to cast everyone. We all have had or will have a villain or villains in our movie. These are the people who show jealousy, put you down, talk bad about you behind your back, lie on you, tell you what you can't do and what your not good at, some are even physical abusers. You don't have to tolerate any of it though. You are basically a Goddess if God made you and you deserve the best treatment. Remind yourself of this when necessary. Believe it or not villains intended purpose is to elevate you. The definition of a villain from dictionary.com is, "a character whose evil actions or motives are important to the plot." So you see, those naysayer, haters, or negative people that don't like you can help you, so appreciate them. They serve a vital role. They do not have permanent roles in your script, nor are they meant to last long in your movie, but they are important. When someone says you can't do something, or hurt you in other ways, learn to focus on the way you can turn that thing around. What purpose can you draw from it? Villains give you something to fight for if you just keep the right perspective. I do not mean fight them physically with your words or physically. I mean, show them better than you can tell them.

Trust me, it will be some of the same people who act like they don't like you, act disinterested in you, and try to belittle you, that really admire you. Some will even copy you and try to get what you have. They may do it directly or in an underhanded way. These same people copy and try to derail you because they see the potential in you and your ideas. The truth is most people do want you to succeed, but not to succeed pass them. No one wants to be left behind or want you to outshine them, especially if they are insecure. And we all have our insecurities. Choose people who have goals, ambition and work ethic to get there as well because they won't fear your rising. I saw a meme recently that spoke to me, it said, "Some people act like they support me, so I act like I believe them." You have to do this with your villains. Don't choose to be close, but when you are around them act cool. Smile and don't let them see that they get to you. Also, learn to protect your vision. Not everyone is worthy of the details and not everyone can go with you. You don't need the negativity dulling your light.

Take time to pick and choose your main characters wisely. I choose to keep minimal contact with certain people, if at all, and I am still working on forgiveness, because I've been hurt. When you believe people are supposed to support you, help you, guide you, and act the part of the roles they are in, it does hurt when they do not live up to it. It is all right though. You got you, God's got you, and new people will fill those roles with time. Sometimes we have to teach and tell others how to treat us and love us, romantic, family, friend, or otherwise. When you give people a script and they just won't follow it, those people need to be cut. Remember that people without boundaries won't respect yours. So don't expect them to. Just find people that fit your goals and be sure to reciprocate showing them love and support` as well. It all gets easier the more you practice healthy boundaries.

You just have to know where to place the cast members on your stage. Don't listen to anyone who wants to put you down and/or dwell on your mistakes. Just learn the lessons from your mistakes. Your mistakes don't define you. And they definitely don't change your status or role in this movie. You are the lead no matter what! You have the full ability to shine as an amazing lead, but you have to choose to act accordingly. I won't play the victim any longer though. I choose to be the victor and my own hero. No one else is set to rescue you or me. God will send help and assistance when necessary, but you are your own hero.

As you hold your casting calls, weeding out the non-talent and highlighting the folks who will make your movie the best yet, answer the following:

1. Are there any relationships that you need to let go of? Why or why not?

2. List the people you trust the most. Why do you trust them?

3. Who is the villain in your script? Why and what purpose d they serve?

4. How are you being honest, open, and transparent with the people in your life? Are they doing the same for you?

5. Who are the people that push you to be your best self? Why? (Even celebrities and social media influencers count).

Chapter 3
Lead Role Preparation

Chapter 3
Lead Role Preparation

Now that we know exactly who the leading lady of this film is, and we are just about sure of who will fill the other major roles, let's talk preparation. How are you planning to reach your goals and dreams? What does it take to get there? A few things you are going to need throughout the process are acceptance, self-awareness, perseverance, resilience, passion, advocacy, and purpose. Let's dig deeper shall we?

First let's discuss acceptance. We must first accept ourselves, flaws and fabulousness, and love all of those same parts. Maybe you wish you could re-do something in the past. You can't, so it is time to forgive yourself and move forward. Now that you are aware, you can make change today, so began. Maybe you wish you were more outspoken like a friend or relative, or more quiet and observant like another. Admire their gifts and personalities, but please honor your own. What are you good at? Honor that. Where do people seek advice from you? Focus there. What comes super easy to you, but others struggle? Cherish that. There is only one you and you are perfect for your purpose. Get out of their movie and focus the lens on yours!

When talking acceptance, we must also accept others as they are. If someone is not as good as you at something, use patience and teach. Or at least accept without judging them. There is more than one way to do most things. So when someone is different than you, appreciate it and move forward. Who knows? Their way may even be better than yours in that area. So keep an open mind. We also need to accept when someone is no good for us and when it's time to move on, instead of wasting time trying to change them.

Moving over to self-awareness. When you are happy, relish in it, lean into what makes you smile. Observe those times and take a moment to realize what works for you. When you are angry, do your best to discover why. Anger is a secondary emotion. So what are you really feeling? Do you feel disrespected, rejected, abandoned, sad, or scared? Write about it, talk to someone you love, and express it to the person, if they can be trusted to show compassion, but get it out. What you don't want to do is block your blessings holding onto hate and anger. Pray, read your Bible, meditate and do what you need to in order to forgive yourself and others. When we don't forgive a part of us stays attached to the person and/or situation. Seek counsel and ask God to help you heal.

I will talk about perseverance and resilience together because it's tough to have one without the other. We need the commitment of perseverance in order to overcome the obstacles that life will give us. We also need to use resilience to bounce back after a set back, when things don't go as planned to keep pushing forward. So whether you want to graduate High School, earn a Degree, have children, raise children to the best of your ability, write a book, get the job of your dreams, start a business, invent something that will change lives, or win the Olympics, there will be times you want to give up. This happens to everyone. It may seem too hard or too far off. If you have the desire though, it is attainable. Those roadblocks come to see how bad you really want it. They come so that you will appreciate the goal that much more once you reach it. Also, then you can teach someone going for it that is coming up behind you. You will be someone's Blessing if you just keep going!

Have you discovered what you are passionate about? What makes you cry? Makes you smile? What makes you say, 'that needs to be changed' or 'this needs to be promoted?' Is there an issue where you find yourself thinking or saying, "They need to do something about that?" Well honey, if you do, that somebody is you. The things that make us tick and we can see a solution for is not the same for everyone else. Also, when you really care and are passionate about something it is easier not to give up. So get a plan together and go be a part of making the change!

It is so important to advocate for yourself and one another when we can. Society is already against females, especially black females, although I think this may be changing. We still need to stand up and speak out against injustice, discrimination and unfairness. Sometimes all we need to do is stand in our truth by living the way we would like society to view us.

I still remember my freshman year, first semester in college. I received my first progress report with my grades; it was looking all right, A's and B's throughout. Only this one C stood out and was hindering my GPA. I was so unhappy with it. Forget unhappy, I was pissed! I could not understand why I received the C. I showed up to every class, I did well on quizzes and the exam, so why? The only thing I could think of is that it was because of my brown skin or that my Professor was using Participation against me. You see it was a Western European History class and that is one subject I just don't care for. It is boring to me and it does not teach the full story of American History, nobody even looked like me. We existed back then! Back to the point though, I needed answers about this C. So I visited the Professor in his office, he was also my Advisor, so that worked out. When I asked him why he thought I deserved a C, do you know that he took a look at the rest of my grades and changed it to a B? See, because I advocated for myself, he understood that I could and would participate in the world, I just chose not to in that class. After this incident we were pretty cool and he mentored me a bit during my college years.

The thing is no one taught me to advocate for myself or I probably would have started this back in High School, lol. What we need to do is teach our girls, well all of our children, to believe in themselves and speak up for themselves at an early age. Then they won't have to learn it later as adults. I was very proud of myself for speaking up for myself and seeing change, so I was able to practice the skill more afterward. I was still very mild mannered with it though. Speaking up became even more prominent after I had my first child. At that point something kicks in, and you realize that you have to protect yourself and your young and it can turn into a mama bear situation, real quick. The only thing is, I would still try to ignore some things and/or be a bit aggressive when I did speak up. At least that is how some took me.

Over time I have learned to be assertive when advocating for my children and myself. I am still learning and practicing being assertive daily. Because when I was a child it was 'Stay in a child's place!' And that place meant be quiet and in your room, or around the corner because my family believed that children were to be seen and not heard. They did their best though based on the tools they were given and I accept that. I just want to change the scenario for my children and hopefully break the chains for a few others. Every one gives kudos to grown women who speak up and advocate for change, but I guarantee those skills were learned and practiced. If kids learn to say no, speak on what they like and don't like now, it won't be as difficult as they grow older to use these skills. They will ask more questions and be better prepared to say no to abuse and discrimination. So lovely, ask questions, it is ok to say no, to speak up, and speak out. Just be sure to be respectful.

My purpose is to change the way that the media portrays girls and woman and how society views us. By uplifting, empowering, and encouraging girls and woman to be their greatest selves, we can create a new generation of positive role models and leaders. The media portrays black women as vindictive, violent, loud, promiscuous, and as caretakers mainly. Those traits may exist, but more than those we are loving, kind, brave, strong, gentle, providers, teachers, and good friends. We need to see this more, which means we need to change this. I used to think, 'They need to do something about this media issue, until I realized that I am a part of the They." Changing the representation of women is a part of my purpose. I can see the clues as I look back from High School on, because every time I had a chance to choose an essay or research topic, the influence of media on women is what I chose. This is where passion meets purpose. I'd like to see a change in the way we are represented in the media to fit how we truly are.

To reach your goals you must strive to always walk in your purpose. When you are not aligned within your purpose, things tend to be harder and you may struggle more. Purpose helps to create flow and when following the script you will have God's grace with you. Not that you will not have your problems while walking in your purpose, because no one is immune, it just makes things a bit easier. You are full of purpose even though you may not always feel like you are. Sometimes your true power just needs to be ignited. Reflect on what brings you joy and past passions to see what you may need to add or strengthen in your life.

If you are honest with yourself you will find strengths as well as weaknesses. Love your strengths and capitalize on them. Your weaknesses are just as important. In your weakness your Director can show His strength. There are issues and limitations you were born with, there may be bad habits you have picked up, and also there are things you just want to improve about yourself. Think about how you can use those same supposed disabilities and limitations to help others. I mean it doesn't matter what it is. You could have been born with a heart problem, one kidney, or a limb missing, but you are here. You have breath and you are functioning, so you have purpose. Someone is going through the same thing, but unable to live freely. How do you still thrive? What can you do to make your life and the lives of others even better? Go do it. Go share it. And maybe your limitation is not as severe, but fear or circumstances disable you. If you were mistreated, abused, bullied, or you just lack confidence due to your personality it's time to work through it. Accept the flaw then become a victor over the issue. You were born into this life with these limitations to show victory. You are a warrior for the cause. Go conquer it!

It's your life, your script, and your show, how it plays out is up to you. You cannot control everything that happens around you, but you can choose your behavior, how you respond, and the next steps you take. Remember things don't happen to you, they happen for you. When life gets rough take it step-by-step, day-by-day, and you will get there. Never try to imitate others because their brand works for them and you have a unique flavor. Study, pray, exercise and better yourself based on your vision, but don't do it for anybody else and don't do any of it trying to be someone else. You are enough to reach those dreams just as you are. Remember to accept yourself, advocate for yourself, study and be aware of your feelings. With perseverance and resilience you can overcome to follow your passion with purpose. So now you must decide how you will lead this film in your role. You may not always feel up to it, but you can do all things! Now go be all of you, all day. I can't wait to see your movie top the charts!

1. What steps can you take to better prepare yourself to lead the movie you dream for yourself?

2. Are you living with acceptance of yourself and others? How

3. Are you self-aware or do you practice self-reflection?

4. How will you perseverance with resilience to reach your goals?

5. What are you extremely passionate about?

6. Do you advocate for yourself and others or will you? How?

7. Are you living within your purpose and with grace? How do you know?

Chapter 4
Setting the Stage

Chapter 4
Setting the Stage

What do you want your life movie to look like? Take a moment to close your eyes and visualize in an ideal world what your life day to day would look like. How does the day start? Who is in it? How does it end and how do you get there? What are your housing, transportation, social life, family structure, travel, hobbies, and career choices? What will retirement look like for you?

For me, I want my lifestyle to flow with my purpose; therefore I've got to be connected. My daily spiritual practice is to read my Bible, talk to God, write in my journal, and plan my day by checking as well as updating my agenda. Some people do better by using their Google calendars and all types of apps, but I'm a paper type of girl, so this is what works for me. I do use Google calendar for most meetings though, it's handy. I also end my day reading the Bible, reflecting, journaling, and with prayer. What I'd like to work up to is increasing my prayer time and meditating at least 15 minutes each day. I will get there as soon as I commit.

As far as setting the scene, my movie is already beautifully chaotic, but it would be a mix of adventure, peace, and glamor. I envision my family living in a 3,500 square foot home sitting on an acre of land (with a fully paid mortgage) having two floors and a finished basement for 2 offices, play space, laundry, and entertaining. My master bathroom is going to be insanely huge with a separate spa tub and stand in shower. I will also have a bidet (Look it up.) I will also own and rent multiple properties. I want to vacation three times per year, once locally in the States and the other times internationally. I'd rather relaxing vacations instead of adventure. I like to sit on the beach, read, watch the children play, and sip on lemonade. Some people want to see all of the attractions, climb, hike, party, and more. That can be fun for me too, but it's not my ideal thing. Occasionally, a visit to the mountains in a cottage can be very relaxing as well. Visiting a few attractions is important to build memories, especially with children, because for me it's all about expanding their view of the world. When I travel, I'd like to fly and stay at an all-inclusive location and/or have drivers, so that there is no 'how to get there' stress for me. Renting a car is cool, but driving for a long time, as well as not knowing where I'm going does something to me. And that something isn't good. Speaking of transportation, I'm not a huge car fan like some who buy three or more expensive cars. I'd like two really nice paid off vehicles, the key is paid off! Lol. One for luxury riding and the other for fun packed family excursions. Actually I'd probably rather a chauffer so I don't have to drive at all, down the line. As you are learning I am not one who loves to drive.

When it comes to hiring folks, I'm big on raising my own kids, but a part time Nanny is up next! Sometimes black women pride ourselves too much on doing it all, which leaves us with no room for ourselves. No! I want that and I'll be a better mother for it. Not just that, but I've always had a vision of doing book tours, fashion shows, interviews and more traveling the country and globe. I knew I wanted children and I did not just want to leave them at home missing me. Now that I have children, I still feel the same. I'd like a trusted Nanny to travel along; therefore I can see them daily. Some people have a mother that can come along, and I don't have that option, but I will gain this luxury.

I'd also like a chef. I can cook and really well, I just don't like to. I'd rather sit and read or play a game with my children. Healthy and delicious meals that I don't have to research for are where it's at! One thing many people want is a maid, but I think I'm good in that area. I can handle it well and have the children chip in to teach them responsibility as well. This may or may not be essential in the future though. I want the option with the choice being up to me. Isn't this movie lit?!

Like what a life! And just to think, I am on my way there. Going for all of it, plus some!

If not home schooled, I want my children to get the best education at some great schools. I want the schools to be diverse with no race left behind. I don't want my children to be the only brown-skinned children in their classes; at the same time I want them to see other children that look different than them. I want them to appreciate the differences of others while also knowing they are to be appreciated for their similarities and differences. My oldest has done karate, ballet, acting classes, and gymnastics programs so I am happy that we were able to put her in those extra curricular activities. Lord knows that they are not cheap. There is so much more that they both want to explore. So another desire is not to have any financial limits on what I can afford to give them access to. In my opinion children need to be exposed to various types of education, museums, sports, and fun activities to learn more about what they are truly gifted at, what they like, and dislike. If you are a mother, or want to be, get those children involved in a variety of activities. If you are a young adult, talk to your parents or guardian about exploring different activities. You will learn so much about your likes and dislikes. This information can help in making career choices instead of waiting until it is time to intern at a place. I sure wish I had these opportunities growing up. I participated in dance, which I loved, but it would have been awesome to have more options. When you know better you not only do better, but you teach better. It is part of my role to expose my children to various opportunities. Because I know how hard it can be financially, one of the many areas I plan to give back in is helping to provide enrichment scholarships for families in need. Our children's futures depend on it.

I've had 9-5 corporate jobs and they were decent, but I always felt limited. What I do love about a job is financial stability. We all need it, don't we? Entrepreneurship is so popular and trendy right now, but it's not for everyone. I've always had an itch to be a business owner, but was resistant thinking about finances, until I was pushed into making it work. Like literally, I was laid off from jobs both times I was pregnant with my children. Both times were in the fall, like in the fall I'm not supposed to work... If that's not a sign... Seriously, how could I really trust depending on a job alone after the second time? Once again, for stability sake, having a job is amazing because bills have to be paid and things need to get done, but for me there has to be a back up plan, just in case. The only downfall to that is if you plan for failure, it usually happens. We have to be careful because we can actually draw things to us at times. I do accept that. Not everything is manifested through us, but some things are. I did not cause those departures though, but I do believe they were ordained. Some people do well in positions for 18+ years, some retire well also, so it really depends on what's meant for you. I want to be in charge of my destiny. So for me being an Author, Encourager, and Empire builder is a choice and a calling.

What is the career or careers you are thinking about for yourself based off of your natural talent, gifts, and education? What do you have to do to get to that life? Do you have to finish High School or earn your Diploma or GED? Go get it! Is it that you need to go to College or a University? Start applying, and get to work! Do you need more experience in your field? It's time to volunteer or intern somewhere to get your foot in the door. Do you need to save more and spend less? If so, it's time to cut back. Is it time to hire help? Do your research, ask for referrals, meet the people and get second opinions if needed. You deserve all of the desires and dreams of your heart. It is time to put a plan into place to receive it.

If you are in college or plan to go to college, be sure to apply to as many scholarships as possible. There are funds available to pay your college bill just for being you. There are some just for girls, for women, by race, ethnicity, based on majors, hobbies, state, city, community involvement and more. Yes there is an application process and you may have to write a short essay, but it is So worth it. I applied to 5 and received 1 throughout my college experience. I left school with my BA $42k in debt. Imagine if I would have applied to 20, 50, or 100 scholarships. I would not have been awarded them all but 1 out of 5 isn't bad. I could have possibly left debt free or close to it.

Why leave school with that burden if you don't have to? Student loans are now one of the biggest reasons that African Americans and other minorities are falling behind and having a hard time getting ahead. Many are busy trying to dig their lives out of debt with a degree, but no great paying job to back it up. Debt is like a prison and I'd rather be carefree.

It won't be easy making the changes needed to get to the next level, but you can do it! To get there you may need to invest in some mentors who are living the lifestyle you'd like to capture in your movie. I say invest because you will most likely have to pay people to take the time to mentor you. You will either pay financially by the hour, through service by volunteering for their cause, and/or by studying their materials such as books, videos, and courses, which may cost time and money. The people around you often need to be on your level or higher so that you can elevate. They at least need to have the ability to encourage you. Mentors are great at keeping you on track and accountable to your goals. If you are really strapped for cash, find someone who understands your journey and may have a similar path. This can be a relative, friend, or network associate. They don't have to be going the same exact route as you, this person just needs to be accepting and understanding of your goals. If you agree, you can be accountability partners. This is a completely free option where you check on each other's progress, give input, and encourage one another as often as you choose. The two of you can create your own check in schedule and tracking system. Be sure to pass the torch by mentoring those coming up behind you.

However you decide to edit your movie is up to you. Adjusting the lens you look through to improve your focus is important to achieve the lasting image you are looking for. It is okay for your vision to change, just get one and start moving toward it.

1. Where do you envision living next year, in 3 years, in 5 years, in 10 years?

2. Do you plan to get married and have children? Why or why not? If you are already married and/or already have children, how can you enhance this area to fit your vision?

3. What type of help do you need to achieve your dreams and goals? What help are you willing to pay for? Plan for it.

4. What certifications, if any, do you need to obtain to reach your goals? How will you pursue them?

5. Do you have a mentor or mentors already? If not, what mentors do you need to add to your circle?

Chapter 5
Behind the Scenes

Chapter 5
Behind the Scenes

For every play and movie you see, a lot goes on behind the curtain and before the Director yells "Action!" Preparing for the performance is not as glamorous as the end result the audience gets to see. This is just about how life is. This is why we should not judge others thinking we're better than them. Nor should we elevate anyone up on a pedestal thinking that his or her life is perfect. Sometimes, we may see others who appear to have it all together, but we don't know what it takes to be them. We don't know the struggles of their day or what they fight with from their past to keep pushing. It is the same with us. We all put on a face to match our roles. When it's friend time we may be open, relaxed and chill, school time we're serious, work time we have a professional face, motherhood time we have to put on our strong superwoman face and cape. When we talk to a parent, close friend, partner, or a counselor we may be able to show the sad, angry, and ugly truth face. I have a game face, you have a game face and so do those you admire. It can be tough being all of these roles at different times and I completely understand your struggle. Just know that you are not alone.

No matter how many hats you wear or how many faces you make, you are enough just as you are. You do not have to pretend. Sure there will be times that we need to be professional, as well as times to censor ourselves. There is a time to play, a time to talk, and a time to listen and be still, but through it all, we also need to be authentic. Authentic means to be true to self and many times that means being vulnerable and transparent. See, I'm learning as an adult that it is ok to be transparent and vulnerable and I am still practicing this skill. This does not make you weak and defenseless. Transparency means being honest and open and it is tough to be transparent without some level of vulnerability. Yes being vulnerable, honest, and open does leave room for you to get hurt and wounded, but what you do in the process is close the door to confusion. If you know that you are being transparent and real, yet you are still rejected or things just don't work out the way you plan, then you can accept that it was not right for you or not the right time. You did your best and was your best, so better is on the way for you. I know I'd rather this versus not giving my all in any given situation and later ask myself "What if?" For example, if we know that we are holding back our love in a relationship and he doesn't act right we may think, 'well I didn't do...' This leaves the door open to unnecessary pain, whether we give others more chances than they deserve to be in the cast, or whether we torture ourselves with woulda, coulda, shoulda. Let's be transparent and know that things happen, as they should. It all has purpose. It is time to come out of hiding. Voice your needs, concerns, and expectations with care and respect.

One of the reasons we hide ourselves is because growing up, our families and society teach us that we must have it all together or at least we must appear to. How is this taught? Some may ask. For boys it is blatant "Men don't cry!" This is even when they are toddlers. That is a baby boy with feelings! I have such an issue with that. The focus here is on females though and some of our girls are getting the message to act grown up as well. It may be that a girl gets hurt and she is told to toughen up. Other times it's 'If you don't stop crying, I'll give you something to cry about.' The thing is, if she is already crying, chances are she already has a reason to. This right here can teach girls not to validate their own emotions. There is a line here though because children will go overboard at times, but know your child and assess yourself to act accordingly. We don't want our children to question if their feelings are worthy because yes your feelings matter and all parts of you are worthy of love, empathy, compassion, and respect.

I did not cry much growing up, but my oldest child did. Most of my aunts and grandmothers guidance was to beat her. I honestly did try a spanking because you just want the crying to stop, but it made it worse, not better. And I just felt guilty and like I was losing my own cool. Instead what she needed was nurturing and to know that she was understood. I mean, crying is not bad. Know that. She needed a person to sit down with her and let her know that she's ok, it's ok, and what she feels matters. My greatest guidance was for her to breath, find out why she's sad, and to use her words. My children can talk and very well, so I always let them know that I am always here with open ears. Letting them know they are not alone is at the root of what usually helps. Other times they may need a little space on their own to figure out their emotions, kind of like adults do. Whether you have been the child in a similar situation or the adult, know that you are just fine. Acknowledge the pain, accept that the people around you are doing their best (even if it is not what you really desire or deserve) and then go continue to do your best.

And ask questions! It is important to your growth. I know that some people may have made you feel as though asking questions was wrong, but it is not. It is necessary. Being inquisitive equals knowledge and knowledge is power. Without you having answers you will just follow the directions of others whether they are right or wrong. In everything, learn for yourself, to know for yourself. If you have felt shut down and shut out, know that it's not you boo, it's them. Yes there is a time and place for everything as well, but you wanting to express yourself and ask questions is fine and you're all right.

Teaching girls to feel or act perfectly is a bit damaging to their true selves, because no one has it together at every moment. The world does enough trying to convince girls and women to be different and better, let's not add to it. We all fall short and make mistakes no matter how young, how old, how rich, how poor, or your skin color. I think mistakes are awesome and are a sign of trying. Just be sure to learn from every mistake you make. Here's what I want you to do. The next time you make a mistake whether it's homework, forgetting something, jumping to soon, saying the wrong thing, or catching feelings for the wrong guy. Instead of beating yourself up, celebrate what you have learned form the experience!

Be on the lookout for folks who try to make your role harder. You're already struggling and they want you to do more. They may not even check in first to see if you can handle it. Unfortunately, something in them may not want you to reach your full potential, so they try to pile more on your plate. Tell them *I don't eat that much.* Their goal is to distract you from your mission and you must stay focused. I know in the black culture we do this far too often, whether intentional or not. We will delegate someone to take care of another relative with or without permission. People expect it and think that you should be ok with it because it is customary to them. If you aren't able to do it, they try to make you feel guilty for not wanting to help. Well no ma'am, throw guilt out the window. You have to take care of self first, or you won't be able to help anyone else. I believe we need to enforce this at a young age.

I've taught my little ladies since they could walk; "You are the boss of your body!" If someone crosses any line you speak up for yourself, defend yourself, and let me know. I even give them options with their clothing and occasionally their food. Sometimes you have to eat what's there and it is what it is, but I try. What this teaches is that they have a say in the decisions in their lives. I don't even make my children hug relatives, myself included. They know to speak and be respectful, but their bodies do not *have* to touch any other person at any time. Young lady, your body is yours. Hug who you choose, smile and greet the rest with words, a high five, or maybe a fist bump. You don't owe not a person in this world, a piece of your body. It is a choice, your choice.

When we learn to put everyone else's wants, needs, and decisions before our own, we learn to take care of others before ourselves. I believe this teaches people pleasing and that we are not that important. We also have to teach and learn how to say no and no thank you. Just because someone offers help or candy does not mean we have to accept it. We can politely decline. If you battle with explaining your no and worrying about offending other people by using your no, it's time to practice. I mean I battle with this. I never had an issue saying no to drugs or alcohol, but with other simple things I didn't think I had reason enough. I'm also a germaphobe, so I've battled with shaking questionable hands and taking snacks from people that I was not sure that I should eat from. I was disappointed with myself when I did not just say "no thank you". For some reason I was caught up in not wanting to offend other people and that is not my style. It did not sit well with me. And I want to respect me, so I had to work on it. So pardon me if I now stand too strong in my no and with no reason or apology. I've practiced and am working on it, and I'm not giving it back. I am teaching and being the example because I want you to walk in your truth now and as you grow as an adult. Practice saying no and yes when you mean it and stand in it. Some may get offended, but that's their problem, not yours. They will get over it.

Do for others when you can and do it out of love. Don't do for others so that they are comfortable even when it causes discomfort for you. Also be sure not to do good deeds while seeking validation or rewards. Do it out of your purpose lead heart. The only place you should look is up to be sure you are making God decisions. The recognition and rewards will come in perfect timing. Therefore, if you are never rewarded by people, you will still be fulfilled because you've been walking in purpose. Some people do have the gift of service and it should be used, but that is not the gift of everyone. With service as your gift, it also does not mean you should help everyone. To me, choices, not forced demands, and putting ourselves first are essential for us to move past people pleasing. If there is anyone in your personal life that really does not care about your needs, then maybe they are trying to take the lead role and need to be cut. Observe them, assess it, and decide for yourself.

True character is built in those moments when you press through doubt to show the world, and more importantly yourself, what you are truly made of. Every time you say "Yes I Can!" instead of saying or thinking 'I can't do this, it's too hard' you are strengthening those can do muscles. This will enable you to go further. This is also how you build self-esteem and confidence. No one can give you self-esteem nor take it away. It is self-esteem for a reason. It comes from within your self. Others have the ability to influence our feelings toward ourselves if we allow them to, but don't give them that type of power. Choose your cast of close folks wisely and rearrange them as needed.

Behind the scenes and closed doors is also where fear resides. We all have fear. What holds most of us back is fear. We sometimes struggle with fear of the spotlight. In the spotlight there is no hiding. In the spotlight all of our flaws are visible. In the spotlight we may fall or make a mistake for everyone to see. That is a scary place because we want to be seen as pretty perfect after all and the spotlight wants to put everything on Front Street. I am a witness to let you know that you my dear can conquer fear even if you fall or forget your lines. Even if you fall, you will heal. If you forget your lines, people may laugh, but you can recover with more practice in the future to have a strong comeback. Never trying on the other hand is the best way not to succeed and the quickest way to make yourself miserable. Not living to our full potential is hard because the calling nags at us. It's just that something or someone along the way convinced us that we might not have what it takes. This may have dimmed our light. That light is still there though, just waiting to burst out!

We have to be self-aware though because sometimes it's not that we are afraid of the spotlight or failure. Sometimes it is our own light that blinds us and we are actually afraid of success and what we could be. Success brings change and change is hard. What does this look like? One visual is, we catch a glimpse of the larger vision and get overwhelmed not knowing where to start. So instead we hide from our gift with busyness to avoid jumping into our true purpose. Blinded. When we are afraid of the change success brings, we doubt and question ourselves. "Who am I to think I can achieve that?", "How will my family and friends view me?", "What will people expect of me?", "What if I look like a phony because I really don't know what I'm doing? I may not be able to keep the jig up." I know that you may have or will some day battle with these questions, because I do myself and I know many others who have as well. This is a normal part of growth. This is also a critical point. Will you break through and say yes while staring fear and doubt in the eye? Or will you continue to stay right where you are? The choice is yours, but your light is there ready to shine whenever you are ready. You are like a lamp and that light is ready for you to flick the switch without worry about what comes next. The Producer and Director in your life, God Almighty knows who and what you need to get there so you need not worry.

The scary part about you forgetting that your light is waiting is, while you may be blinded by your light and at a stand still, there are people around you who can see your light, and vividly. Some will see the light within you, guide you, back you, and do what they can to support you. Then there are others who recognize the light and don't like it so they try to destroy you. People will use lies, slander, gossip, and other distractions to attempt to keep you entangled with them at their level. Try to remember that when people treat you poorly it is a reflection of them and has nothing to do with you. If anything they want you to receive the negativity, so that you can doubt yourself and not go forward in the role God has given you. These are distractions. Don't get off track!

Do not take any persons demeanor or words personally. I repeat Do Not receive their negativity. Any time someone tries to bring you down hit the return to sender button in your mind! That's for them, not you. Happy, successful, and valuable people spread love and happiness. Those bitter folks spread their bitter germs. Let them have it, don't join in. Many people are happy and supportive of you until they think you are about to leave and outgrow them. They can't handle that, but that's not your problem.

I know that I was afraid to say no and afraid to succeed. I've learned that it's ok to say "No" and if people don't like it they'll get over it. Most people will understand if they show care for themselves and if they truly care and support you. So if you really are wearing yourself thin with too much on your plate, or it's something you just don't want to do, just say no. I was also afraid thinking that some would judge me saying, "Who does she think she is?" I'm learning daily, but I am so happy that I can put a *was* on it! Now, I am ready for every Blessing and great opportunity coming my way. The judge still jumps up from time to time, but I'm able to ask her to take a seat because I've got the floor. I am ready to let go of my now to get to my greater. Are you ready for that? I hope so, because it's show time!

1. What is something you learned about being female growing up that may be stunting your growth mentally, emotionally, and/or financially? What can you do about this?

2. Who do you talk to when you really need to be heard and understood? Who are you helping by showing you understand them?

3. Are you afraid to be your true self in any area of your life? If so, which one? How can you conquer this?

4. Who are you behind the scenes that you need to bring to the stage? What's stopping you?

5. What are you afraid of people knowing about you? How can you learn to love this part of yourself and use it to your advantage?

6. Write about your most recent mistake and what you learned from the situation. Then add how you celebrated or will celebrate it.

Chapter 6
The Squad

Chapter 6
The Squad

What do the movies *Girls Trip, Set It Off, Bring It On, Cheetah Girls, and Descendants* have in common? Other than amazing plots and record numbers in the box office and views on television, they all include a level of sisterhood. It's the type of sisterhood we all sort of crave. We want to know that there are a few ladies that have our best interest and if it goes there we have their backs as well. Sisterhood is important and powerful. As females we are intelligent, intuitive, brave, and creative. With these super powers there is nothing we can't accomplish when we decide to work together.

I don't know about you, but I've always been a bit jealous of the way guys acknowledge each other. They don't have to know each other and they still give each other a head nod to say, "What's up bro." The experience for females can be totally different. We will walk right past each other without a word or glance. Why is this? I believe what stops us from really loving and supporting each other usually comes down to jealousy and insecurity. We need to stop this because there is enough for us all. Some of it is passed down, but we have the ability to change it. Use the stories, triumphs and accomplishments of other ladies to inspire you. Because they are doing it or have done it, you can too! It is my dream that we will raise a generation of girls who will bond, build, congratulate, and encourage one another other. To get there though, we must live it. They have to see it. So I make it my mission to uplift other females. This can be through a post on social media, a compliment about their looks, accomplishments, or praise for a job well done. I notice my daughters saying how pretty a girl or woman's dress or outfit is and it makes me proud! They had to get it from somewhere. They get it from their mama! Let us all pass the love to others and down to ours for them to spread love as well.

Getting compliments and conversations from males is awesome! It's something about another female acknowledging us though. After all, a guy may have another motive because he's after the gift. When it is a female, it can feel very genuine, build a bond, and even a close friendship, as long as there is no funny business going on (and most times it's not). With this said, let's say hello to other girls and women. And when someone speaks to you, say it back! You can even go a step further when you are loving her hairstyle, shoes or jacket. Let that girl know. Sometimes we may fear rejection. What if she does not speak back? The good thing is, most people will respond. For the ones who don't remember you are doing this out of the goodness of your heart and not to please them. If it uplifts them, great! If they are a sourpuss and are not fazed, that is not your department. You did a good deed, move forward and repeat. Be sure to smile when you say hello! You never know, you may be brightening someone's day, gaining a new friend, or business associate.

Friendship can be awesome! Having someone to laugh with, play with, cry with, go to the mall with, go on trips with, talk about fellas with, and who does not judge you is awesome. When you are young you want a lot of friends to have fun with. As you grow older, your circle gets smaller because having meaningful friendships matter more. It becomes quality over quantity. Actually, no one needs friends anymore. We now have fans and followers, that's what matters. LOL!!! That was so hilarious to type. OMG! Social media is something else. That statement was so untrue though. It is great to build a brand and a following, but most of those connections aren't real. We can all use at least one good true friend. That's all you really need is one or two who will be there in times of need. When you are confused or sad they are there to talk. When you are bored they are ready to hang. When you are really going through they will pray for you, check on you, and try to lift you up. Some friends will be ready to fight or tell off another human being for you because they have your back and your front. Hold on to them, but you

56

may have to give them guidelines. Some show care more or different than others, but being there for each other, that's what friends are for.

Sisterhood can begin when we stop judging, belittling, competing, and being jealous of each other. If she can do it or get it, you can do it too. It may be a different way, but you have your own lane. Pull each other up and share resources. There's no need to be stingy. The only thing you don't have to share is your children and your man. I'm not sure how some people can sleep with someone else's man knowingly and say they are for sisterhood. When you do so you are hurting another female.

Truthfully, one reason we don't trust each other is because some females are sneaky and they think it's cute. I'm not sure what's attractive about being a- in Monica's words- "Sideline Hoe". You may get sex, maybe a few meals and gifts, but no real quality time. He won't be available on Holidays and can't hold you down when it counts. It may be fun and a thrill in the moment, but there are a few things to think about: 1. What will you do when you're lonely, but he can't answer his phone and can't come to see you? At these times he is spending time loving on his wifey and/or kids. Side chicks even catch feelings and get their feelings hurt, but it's what you sign up for in that role. You're waiting on him, but he's not really leaving her, and you could be building a real life with a single and free man designed for you. 2. If he's cheating on her with you, there is a 99% chance he will cheat on you. He's probably cheating on his sidepiece with an appetizer. So no, it's not just the two of you, but others and you are putting yourself at further risk of catching sexually transmitted diseases and STI's. Respect and protect yourself too much for that.

I remember a situation in my early 20s where my boyfriend was cheating and I called a girl for more information (Never again, just dump him). Any who, she was knowingly a side chick because she did not even have his real name or number. But can you tell me why she was mad at me because I had questions? So she knowingly put herself out there, hurt another sister, and did not care about any damage done? That's sad. Not for me, I'm over it, but some females have no compassion or respect for themselves and others. We can say men are dogs all day, but without the opportunities they can't carry out actions. This is why it can be hard to trust each other. Let's do better ladies!

I can now many times feel a connection to another sister and it's just a question of where and how do we mesh? Where can we partner? I can now usually tell whom I can trust because we are vibrating on the same frequency. We both have goals, plans, and are making marks. We both have things to lose and gain. I don't trust too many stagnant, same ole type females. They sometimes want your life- your funds, dreams, and man included.

As you get older you learn who your true friends are and not. Sometimes you will lose friends, but you will also gain some down the line. After tough experiences and being let down, you may even trust people less. This doesn't make for quick friendships, but if you're open to it, new bonds will form. Just keep trusting that gut and your past experiences. I know I don't have as many friends as I used to. I am a highly functioning introvert. Although I am able to socialize, uplift, empower, and I'll start a party when my song comes on, I am definitely all in all an introvert. I enjoy me time, alone, quiet, or doing what I like. I've always had friends, but it's usually people who gravitate toward me. Most have always been good friends. The thing about having light is that you draw positive and negative to you. Light attracts light, but the darkness is drawn too. So you have to be careful and discern who is for you and not. Sometimes you know from the gate and other times you have to wait and watch. People will show themselves. Just don't ignore the signs.

I no longer have a ton of close friends because over time people have moved, I have children, many of my long time friends do not, some people still love to party, and it's not my every weekend theme any more, so you lose touch with folks. To remain close friends you have to keep in contact. It's hard to keep in contact when your values and interests change due to status change, whether this change is marriage, parent, or single. If your anything like me, people want to be your friend and that is how you gain or have gained them. As a youth this was usually true for me. As I grow though I notice that I do have to work harder to gain and maintain friendships. This is good though; it forces me out of my shell. So no matter how old or young you are, never be too good or too shy to make a new friend. Friendships take consistency and dedication. When you are little there are play dates, then sleep overs, then hanging at the mall and movies, then power lunches, phone-a-thons (on the phone for hours), and sometimes business partners.

When you enter into a meeting, a room, or collaboration go with an intention. You may not have all of the right words to say, but go with confidence and a goal. When I first stepped out on faith more on social media, I had people reaching out to me to meet, connect, and collaborate. The problem was that I would attend these meetings and gatherings and leave excited that they wanted to meet with me, but with nothing learned or gained. So in essence, I wasted my time. I went with thoughts like, "I'm so special that they want to meet with me" and "I wonder what they want to know or what they'd like from me". So I answered many questions and maybe asked a few of myself, but I really left empty handed. See, no one taught me how to network. What I learned is that I need an intention going in. So now I decide what I'd like from others, how they can help me, and how I can help them. If you don't decide for yourself in this life, there are plenty of people who will decide things for you. Now I leave with a plethora of knowledge, a new business partner or collaboration, and maybe even a new sister-friend. You have to do the work first though and decide your purpose in life so that when you invite others into your bubble, they serve a purpose. It is not using because you will offer a support for them as well. #Teamwork and #SistahBuilding

If you take a look around you can see the power of women. We are taking over! Women are CEO's Entrepreneurs, mothers, lawmakers, and change agents. Imagine if we really pulled together. Not just on social media and business, but in every area. Our schools, communities, businesses, boutiques, restaurants, events, and more would flourish further. I think we are headed there, but we can do more. It is ok to go it alone to get there quickly, but if you want to get there with strength, it will eventually take a team. With this said, let's stop reinventing the wheel. If you see a girl, woman, or organization doing what you want to do, do not give up on your dreams, instead join forces. You can also still create your own lane doing the same thing on your own if you like because your styles and purpose are different. You may pull in two separate audiences doing the same thing. There is space for us all. The reason I say join together, whether locally or internationally, is because there are so many people hosting the same types of events and starting the same type of company and organizations. If we collaborate and build together, we can build larger powerhouses. We can create more diverse Fortune (500+) corporations by pooling our funds, resources and brains together. You do have to be smart when gaining partnerships, but it can be done. Use discernment, never forget to agree, sign and keep contracts, and date before jumping into full partnership. I am not insinuating that you date romantically. What I mean is meet a few times for dinner, tea, or power lunches. Get to know this person and maybe run a small project together first to see how well you work together. If you choose people with the same values and interests, you may be a great fit or you may need to find someone else, but find out.

Sisters, black, white, tan, yellow, red, and purple, we need each other. Let's raise these babies, these schools, these businesses, and communities together. Protect each other by doing your research on these guys you date to be sure he's not about to break both of your hearts. And don't be one of those ratchet sideline hoes that try to have sex with other ladies men purposely. Hold yourself to a higher standard than that. If you don't know you deserve the best, meaning being the only one in a fella's life, then it's time to re-evaluate yourself and affirm greatness over yourself. Refer back to Chapter 3 if needed, because you do not need to settle to be a side order. You are a full meal my dear. Ladies, be sure to say hello, give a smile, and compliment other girls or women regularly. Many times we think it, but don't say it. Let's say it, even through the fear. It may really change a girl's day. Let your goal be to speak your truth and empower, because even if she can't receive it, you are living bravely as a positive example.

1. What does sisterhood mean to you?

2. Who do you consider to be a part of your squad? With their names right why?

3. Who is always there for you in a time of need? Tell them thank you today via text, phone call, or in person.

4. Who are you there for when help is needed? How do you show that you are trying to be a great friend?

5. Are there any girls or women you'd like to collaborate with? If yes, who and to partner on what? How can you approach them?

6. If you are looking to gain more friends, what are a few ways that you can start this process?

Chapter 7
On the Set

Chapter 7
On the Set

Sometimes we have to get out of our own way. Not taking a leap or stepping out on faith, waiting for opportunity to come to us, and depending on others, holds us back. You have a major role on this Earth and it's waiting on you to fulfill it. Sure there will be folks who don't believe in you or your vision and you may receive a thousand no's. The thing is, *all* you need is *one* yes, because a force much bigger than you is orchestrating it. You being born when you were, into the family you were, and the environment was no accident. You have a grand purpose to fulfill. You coming 100 years ago or 100 years from now were not options because you are needed for this moment in time. If you are walking in your purpose, keep pushing through the good and the struggles. If you don't believe you are yet walking in your purpose it's cool, you can start today. It won't always be easy, but you can. You can begin right now! You are the lead character and whom you surround yourself with is crucial to the plot.

They say you can determine your success, by the 5 people closest to you. If the people around you motivate you, challenge you to be better, and are successful themselves (or at least going towards it) then you are walking with the right group. If the people around you are bitter, vengeful, complainers, complacent, or gossipers, it's time to replace a few crewmembers. Every movie has a full line up: The lead role or main character, major cast members, the villain(s), and a captivating plot. Behind the scenes are writers, producers, a director, videographers, and more. And it is my belief that most major films have God on their team as a Director. He can get you further than you ever could alone, so I dare you to partner up! Not everyone believes in the name God, but Allah, Jehovah, Higher Power, The Universe, and most other religions/ beliefs all have similar principles. It's the energetic source above and beyond. God is my choice. To me He is the only choice. It is your faith in what you believe that will matter and get you through.

How is it on the set of your life right now? Is it quiet, full of drama, or action packed? Who is bringing each element? When do you feel the most at ease and at peace? Who are you around when you feel you can accomplish anything? I ask these questions to help you determine who should step up to main characters, if they are not already. On the other hand, those that drain your energy, criticize you, cause you to cry, or cause insecurity, and if they are always combative should be Extras if they cannot be replaced all together. Even those villains can serve a purpose. We just need to know when their roles expire. What I've decided for myself is everything is negotiable, except peace! We can talk and discuss anything and come to a compromise, but not when it disturbs my inner peace. It is hard to think straight without peace. I need to be able to think straight in order to make proper decisions and to be effective.

Some situations are tougher than others to get away from. In the work place, for example, it can be hard to tolerate a cruel supervisor or an obnoxious co-worker. We have to pay those bills; so quitting without a plan is usually not an option. Just stay prayed up and try to be optimistic. Hopefully someday your positivity will rub off on them. In the meantime seek other positions and believe it will work out. I get that there are going to be people like caregivers and other relatives that you may not be able to get away from as quickly as you'd like. Just pray through it knowing that you will grow through it, even with those individuals. Remind yourself that this is a temporary scene and you have so many more to go. As you get older you may understand some of these adults that baffle you as a child, realizing that they meant well. Other times you can look forward to the days when you are able to provide enough for yourself to be on your own and hosting a new casting call.

Sometimes the folks who show to be our biggest enemies are our relatives. This is a sad truth because they are the ones that should have our back and root for us the most. Right?! It just does not always go this way. The most jealous people can come in the form of family and their betrayal does hurt more than most. I know some people who have great loving relationships with their relatives and this is awesome and how we should all strive to be. It is beautiful. If you have a very supportive family, appreciate them and be as loyal as you can without betraying yourself, because it is a blessing. Be sure to thank them. If on the other hand, you have experienced family, friends, or foe that talk about you, lie on you, who are unsupportive, who are jealous and hateful, etc., just pray for them. Distance yourself, remove them from the plot as far as you can, and keep pushing. Don't allow yourself to stick in toxic environments due to familiarity, family, friend, romance or foe. It's unhealthy and uncomfortable.

I've been there. I even had to walk away from some of my relatives. And I am big on family! See, we were evicted a couple years back and needed a place to stay for a few months. I was so happy that my Grandmother said yes and opened her home to us. During this time, there were some relatives who caused all types of chaos and confusion. Instead of trying to help with encouragement, advice, support, or offering a hand, they talked about me, my children, and husband behind my back, spread lies, and thought up vicious plans. They could not get them to pass though. I was reminded that God never said the weapons wouldn't form. He said they wouldn't prosper. Don't forget that. I mean it got so bad that one of my aunts literally tried to get my family kicked out of my Grandmothers house, the only place we really had to go. And to think it was all over petty kid squabbles that could have been resolved with adult communication and support. I had to find out so much from other people instead of the source. While we were already going through trauma over eviction, people had the nerve to add drama. I still have a hard time believing that people can stoop that low. Like, talk to me, communicate with me and let me know what's going on because maybe we can solve this. How can we work together? That's how I function. But you will learn that not everyone thinks or operates like you.

They cut me deep. If it wasn't bad enough that I don't have the support of my mother (she passed away in 1998) they showed me that I could not count on them either. They chose to throw daggers, instead of lend a hand of assistance. When people are older than you with more experience, you expect them to teach and guide you. I am still working on forgiveness because that is very important, but I also now know when to cut ties with people. So that's what I had to do. For my sanity and to keep my children from experiencing unnecessary pain, I have to keep a distance. It is ok to love people from afar. I believe that whole-heartedly. Some people would let it go and say 'oh it's just family, that's what they do, they talk'… But honey, no! Not the family that I will choose to be surrounded by. When I spend my precious time with people, it will be because they are encouraging me or I will be encouraging them. It is great that I am finding so much love from women locally and around the world that have similar missions as I do. Those are my *Squad Goals* that I'd like to call family and hang with. My time is expensive and I can't get a second back, so I choose to spend it wisely. My dear, I suggest you do the same.

Realizing that cutting some people off, is easier said than done when we have ties and bonds, take it day by day and gradually lessen time spent. Some people you may opt to deal with in doses. That's a 'hey, how you doing?' Quick hug, pat, pat and keep it moving type of thing. I'm not saying that everyone and every situation is deserving of cutting ties with. If it is miscommunication, a one-time mistake, one disagreement, someone that you were really close with and they thought they were looking out for your best interest, talk about if first to see if there is anything worth salvaging. You may be able to come to a compromise or understanding.

When I speak of moving people out of your cast, I am speaking on the ones who just like drama and don't really want to talk to discuss a solution. Talking about the ones that are unsupportive or talk down in regards to your ways or dreams. Speaking on those that you feel worse about yourself instead of better when in their presence. Get away from those when you can, no matter who they are.

One thing I learned about people is that successful folks don't have time to talk, gossip, and bring others down. Successful people are too busy adding elements to their movie to see if anyone else's has graphics or who's is only in black and white. Successful people also have the ability to uplift and encourage because they have received it and/or needed it before as well. Miserable people just want company; so encouraging another does not fit into their agenda.

To get to that next level you will have to leave some people behind, it is required. You can do it because your future depends on it. Then once you distance yourself you have to do something else even more difficult. That is, you must forgive. Forgive them because they are really just showing how much pain they are in themselves. Ask God to forgive them and let His will be done, because they didn't know they were messing with His child. And most of all forgive yourself. Letting ourselves get treated particular ways and putting ourselves in harm way is painful and needs healing. Keep loving you boo. You are only human. You are still amazing through it all. Don't hold on to it. Just part ways as a form of love to yourself.

With that, I'd like to add that you just being you without actually hurting others can't make people dislike you. You don't even have the power to make people like or love you. It's all up to individual preference. There will always be people who like and show support to you and there will always be some who don't care for you. That is not your business. Just keep doing you and your tribe will appear. You will get called into the right circles and things will happen in a flow.

You are on the set of the most anticipated film in years! You are unable to go back in time to make changes like they do when making real movies, so give it your all, do your best, and cancel the rest. When you recognize mistakes or things you can do better is yell "cut!" to yourself and reflect on lessons learned to take them forward and make magic.

It doesn't matter who your family is, parents are, or what they have done, become, or not, nor does your upbringing matter. You my dear *Can* do anything you put your mind to. Easy, hard, and in- between, You Got This! And if you decide not to give up, you *Will* succeed. Who is your Fab 5? Or who *will* they be? Let's clean up the set!

1. Write down the 5 people you spend the most time with. How does each of them make you feel?

2. How are your family dynamics? Is it healthy or unhealthy? Why?

3. If you need to cut family or a previous lover out of your life or have done so before, what is the most challenging part and how will you overcome that? (Because you will Overcome it!)

4. List 5 people that you can get to know and create bonds with. Why those people?

Chapter 8
Wardrobe & Beyond

Chapter 8
Wardrobe & Beyond

Chapter 8
Wardrobe & Beyond

What is a movie without wardrobe and costumes? Right?! The way each character looks sets the scene and illuminates their personalities. Did you know that people get an opinion about you within 5 seconds of seeing you? This is before you even open up your mouth to speak. I'm not saying this is fair or that people will always be completely correct, but this is how our brains work. Once a person communicates with you, they will judge their own accuracy and choose whether or not to engage further. I'm sure to some degree you do the same. Because we need to be able to trust ourselves, I guess this is fair and we should use our own discretion along with our God given intuition when dealing with others.

Clothing, cleanliness, and style are important parts of our package. The greatest thing I want to stress here is to be sure to dress for the role you want. If you are looking for a job or going on an interview you should wear a nice blouse, preferably a button up top with a pair of nice dress pants or a knee length skirt. Add a blazer or sweater and be sure that all is wrinkle free. If you are hanging out with friends and family, a nice tee with jeans might be an awesome choice. In all of this, how you choose to wear your hair is a choice completely up to you. Some swear by the bundles, weaves, and wigs, others are relaxed and laid, and then others are au natural. Whatever your choice, rock it! Wear what suits you, not what is popular or trendy.

In my opinion natural hair is on trend right now, but it is not my thing. If it is your thing, work it girl! I do agree that natural hair can be very beautiful, but managing 4C coils daily, is not for everyone. I did try it, but did not love the look or the maintenance. I only gave it one month and was back to a relaxer. See, I have two daughters and I have to keep all 3 of our heads on point. Nobody has time to curl and prep every night to look like something the next day. A relaxer allows me to brush my hair around and wrap it up. It is a very quick process, even with rollers. I love a nice neat and quick look. I really would love to get up and go! We all have preference. I don't love using chemicals, but there are far worse things in the world. No matter what your choice is, don't let anyone shame you into thinking you should change your style and choices. Wear what makes you feel beautiful. Your skin and experience does not change due to hair texture or color change. Tell them to get a life. If you want purple hair, red hair, blue, green, or rainbow hair, you go for it! I prefer black and relaxed, so this is what I rock. One thing I may do someday is transition into Sisterlocs. I love the look as well as the versatility, and it's easy maintenance. Goals!

Like India Arie said, *"I am not my hair"*. I am also not my clothes, but I do choose to dress appropriately. Let me give you a few more tips. If you want to attract a nice good guy, willing to wait for sex with you, ditch the mini skirts, skintight clothing, cheek revealing shorts, and cleavage popping tops. What I just listed are booty call clothing items. To get the attention of a male while letting him know you expect respect, dress in clothing that covers your assets. It is ok to wear fitting clothing because you can turn heads with your clothes on boo. You are beautiful enough to do so. If you do this already, Go girl! If you don't yet, try it! Where your true beauty will shine is in your hair, makeup, how your clothes fit (dress for your body type and age), your smile, and most of all your personality.

When I was a new mom, I remember taking my daughter to the park to play and it felt so different. Not just being a mother, but feeling naked. See, I had on booty shorts (really short shorts) and I felt violated every time someone looked at me. So I can't pretend that I have never worn little shorts, tight clothes, and cleavage revealing clothing before because I have. I did not dress this way all of the time, but I did occasionally. Needless to say, those shorts got a new home. Now I understand what my aunts and grandmother saw and criticized. In my teens and early 20's I thought they were just out of date with style and didn't know any better. But now that I am older and see young girls, I completely get it.

If your goal is to be the girlfriend or wife, prepare for that role while single and as you date. You are a gift darling and the guy worth it will most likely like his gifts wrapped. That means fully dressed darling. Most boys and men don't want to invite the hoochie over to meet their parents, and they won't. They'll sneak a hoe around to have sex, but not to stick around. Don't be her. Dress for success in all areas. Your role is Queen! Act like it and don't forget it!

Watching music videos and much social media content will lead people to believe that it is cool, cute, and sexy to dress provocatively. The saying still holds true that 'sex sells.' People will pay for sex, pay to watch sex and many enjoy watching the female body indecently exposed however and whenever possible. Because I am the lead and I have a plan, I choose not to be entertainment for others sexual gratification. My goods are for my husband only. Our bodies are beautiful so there will be some who lust no matter what we wear, but I'm not here to make it easy.

And the music nowadays is so disrespectful! We can be mad, but the bigger problem here ladies, is that we co-sign by being a part. There are women in these videos barely clothed by choice, we buy the music, watch the videos, etc. We are called B's, hoes, one of their many thots, referred to as the thick chick and more. We are referred to as objects in most rap songs. We are even objectifying ourselves in our own music nowadays. It is horrible! Then we get surprised when we are treated this way by the boys and men in our lives. This is their example because the media and music has influence. I know we can't change everything, but we can hold ourselves accountable to how we dress, how we are treated, and what we decide to participate in.

To protect yourself, be abstinent, choose wisely, use condoms, use birth control, and decide what others will see. We are in a digital age where everyone is posting pics on social media and some are inappropriate. Remember that these are public platforms and open to the world. Unfortunately others can use these images, a company will view them before hiring you, and you want to appear as your best self even on social media because it represents you. Yes you are attractive and want to look appealing, but not like a piece of meat. This brings me to texting, or shall I say sexting. Here's a good rule of thumb, don't do it! There are too many boys and even grown men who may try to use these images in the wrong way. They may show their buddies, post them, or may go as far as blackmailing you if you don't give them what they want. No thank you! Screw that. It has happened and may continue. I just hope you can stay away from that trap. If he is worth it, eventually he will see the goodies in person. Let him know this. Are you afraid that he will lose interest or find another girl to do what he asks instead? Well you are right to feel this way, because he may. The thing is, he may search for her whether you comply or not, so seek your best interest love. If you have already done this, forgive yourself and be sure not to send another undressed photo. If you receive threats, let him know that you will be happy to take this information to the police department. Be prepared to follow through if he keeps harassing and/or actually shares or posts an image of you. If you are under the age of 18 he can get hit with some pretty major charges dealing with child pornography. Most guys don't want that, so let him know your angle and get far away from him. People like that do not deserve second and third chances.

Let's do some house keeping. As much as you are able, keep your hair neat and face clean. Make your bed, do your chores, and keep your house clean. Be sure to clean those under arms and wear deodorant that lasts. Keep your private areas clean and don't douche. You are clean enough down there already. Douching promotes the growth of fungi and bacteria causing your body to depend on douching. Eat fresher food and air dry when possible. Always carry a pad or panty liner with you just in case. It may come in handy for you or a friend. I also carry vaginal wipes to freshen up, especially when it's hot. Another tip to stay and smell fresh is to brush your teeth three times a day for real, once in the am, another after lunch, when you get out of school or work, and then at bedtime. Keep those cavities, germs, and bad breath away. Let's keep this fresh image going. You don't have to by particular name brands or certain labels to look good. Just rock what you feel good in. Always be neat in your appearance and be on time if not early for attendance, meetings, and appointments. Being consistent with all of the above will speak volumes of your character.

Your goods should be like classified information, hard to get access to. Can anyone walk into the white house on any given day to see the paintings, rooms or private affairs just because they feel like it? I think not. And not everyone has been inside of Oprah's mansion. And you young lady need to be treated with this same high regard. Anyone that looks at you should not be able to see your goods with a glance. As the saying goes, "leave something to the imagination". You are judged by the way you present yourself. I need you to understand that if you dress in skimpy clothing you appear easy and you have a higher chance of being disrespected. Other females may view you as a slut, young boys will talk to you with the intention to get into your panties only, and rumors may begin, then spread like wild fire. To add to this you are less trusted around friends and relatives, and it would be difficult to get a job dressed inappropriately.

When you look at celebrities like Yara Shahidi, Michelle Obama, MsBling, Chloe and Hailey Bailey, Mary Mary and many more you will see that they are very popular, beautiful, like to have fun, are successful, and they dress respectfully. How is this possible? They are true to themselves. They refuse to sell out for sex. They love their bodies and they know that they have greater purpose than being a sex symbol. I'm with #FullyDressedAndKillingIt. Are you?

I've always had concerns with the way girls and women were portrayed in the media. Like I stated before this was my go to topic for research papers. So I knew my role would be to increase a diverse array of imagery for girls and women. This means race, color, size, and shape. It also refers to demeanors, actions and attitudes. Girls and women are so complex. We are full of strength, attitude, and perseverance. We are also full of peace, grace, and optimism. This is for all races and it needs to be showcased more often.

I believe that if enough girls and women decide to dress and carry themselves with class, we can lead a generation of girls on a positive path as role models. Let's show them that class is back, because it is! Smart is the new sexy and knowledge is our super power, so let's keep our eyes in the books and stay informed. #TeamTurningHeadsFullyCovered

1. What types of clothing give you a confidence boost? Why do you think that is?

2. What types of clothing are you against or uncomfortable wearing? Why?

3. What kind of statement do you want to make to the world with you image?

4. If you had unlimited funds to buy a new wardrobe, what would your style look like? Is there a celebrity that embodies your style?

5. How do you feel about the role of girls and women in the media? What would you change if you could?

Chapter 9
The Romantic Scene

Chapter 9
The Romantic Scene

If I only knew then what I know now... I understand that statement now. Do you? I have made many decisions in my 34 years, good and bad, but I am happy that I've also learned a lot. There is no point in going through, learning a lesson and not teaching it to others. So everything I am sharing I have experienced myself or known someone who has personally. I realize that I am such a treasure now. I've always known this, but I guess at times I forgot. Young lady you are God's gift to man and to this world, never forget that. God made Eve because Adam needed help, not the other way around. There is a man out there that *needs* you. These little boys don't know what they want, let alone need, and many are just plain old selfish. A boy will make his girl feel jealous, a man will cause other women to be jealous of his girl. Which one do you prefer? Maybe you are only a teenager and Man sounds old. Maybe you are right when related to age, so I am not saying go out there and start dating older men. What I am saying is choose someone who values what you do and is going your direction. We females mature faster than they do so we have an advantage, but we have to let logic lead until he shows to be worthy of your emotions as well. Males are born hunters, so you should know if he is serious or not. If he seems disinterested then maybe he is. No one is busier than a guy who is not interested or committed to you. We all have the same 24 hours in a day and we make time for what we choose to.

I sure wish I had this information sooner, like 20 plus years ago. I would be so much further along if I had not spent so much time chasing someone to love me the way I wanted. Asking for attention, care, and communication, instead of running after my goals. Wondering why he lied, cheated, and would he do it again? That should not have been my business! I should have voted him off the cast the first time. I feel for that young woman I was and I am still healing past it because it takes time and there was a lot of trauma. Sometimes we are so into the fairytale of what could be that we are not realizing our reality. So lady, be more focused on your growth, protecting your mind and goals than on any guy. Believe me, no one is worth it.

It is very interesting that puberty is beginning for both males and females at alarmingly early ages, which means hormones are raging out of control. You may be very curious about kissing, touching, oral pleasure, and actual intercourse. That is ok. It can be pleasurable as well as very painful. Ask trusted people questions. Some information is that having your menstrual cycle means that you can now carry life. So please honor your temple. Having a child is a gift and a beautiful thing, but you really want to be ready mentally, emotionally, as well as financially because having a child is also a huge responsibility. Not too much costs more than raising a child, especially if you want the child to experience the world. Starting your menstrual cycle as well as just being a female means that you can get pregnant and have a child of your own. Decide if you are ready for that and make decisions accordingly.

The best thing to do is to have your career and finances in order before getting serious with any guy. That way if you decide to part ways you are not dependent upon him and what you had together. This means, if you decide to have children you will have the means to support you and any child(ren). There are plenty of systems to help, but you will feel so much more confident knowing that you have it under control. Now mind you, you can plan until your thoughts run dry and things can still fall apart, but at least you have a greater chance of not being a struggling single mother if you make decisions accordingly.

Romantic relationships are important though and that is why this is the longest chapter in this book. I am not saying just don't date, don't like guys or any of that. What I am saying is keep you as a priority. Your Co-Star can help to build you or break you. You are the leading lady and the guys you date are supporting cast members. They need to support the vision of your life fully in order for it to run smoothly. So protect yourself physically and mentally. Physically use condoms and birth control and mentally be sure you feel good about you when dealing with a guy. Choose a guy who honors and respects you, one who does not leave you wondering. I don't know what it is that makes us want a guy who is unavailable. It may be our absent daddy void that we are trying to mimic and fill. It may be that we think we can change people, but we can't and people aren't projects. Or it may be the media because many of those role models don't scream faithfulness, loyalty, and care for women, or it may be a mixture of all of these things. What I do know is that chasing a partner is not our role. The male is the hunter.

The male is also a leader, teacher, and has the ability to commit. Trust me if you have to chase him in the beginning you are signing up to do that for a long haul. Men don't change because you have his children. Most men don't even change because they are married. A boy or man changes when he is ready to because change starts from within. You though darling cannot change him. It's not your job. We weren't made to change others. You want a whole boy or man who wants a whole one girl or one woman, so only commit to that. What I am also not advocating is to go out here and sleep around with Terry, Joe, Mark, or Stacey as an excuse not to be committed to just one guy. Your body is a temple, so treat it as such. What have they done to deserve the cookies? Does he give you money or buy you things? I f yes, good! He should, as a part of his role, but you can do that for yourself if you choose, so it does not mean you owe him that type of gratification. Save your goodies for the guy who doesn't make you wonder and knows how to make your day better. The good guy who can put a smile on your face, be faithful, is consistent, wants to communicate and solve problems together, and has ambition, that's the one darling. That's what constitutes a great partner.

'Does he love me?' Or Does he care?' These are questions we all ask at one time or another as we are questioning a guy's motive. You may feel infatuated and in love with him and you want to know that he feels the same. Instead of wondering how he feels, I am challenging you to decide that he does love you. Whether he tells you he loves you, you want him to love you, or you are just unsure, tell yourself he does. The reason why I say this is because it does not matter if he loves you. What does matter is how he makes you feel. Whether he loves you or not his behavior (over time) is a clear indicator of his intention. A guy who you don't have to waste time agonizing over like, 'Will he call? Why didn't he call? Is he going to apologize? Will I ever see him again?' That one, he's not the one, unless you like drama. The one for you will call, text, and check in on you daily. There are some jerks that will do the good things for a little while as well, so stay watchful and look for consistency. He could also love you and treat you well, but you are just not feeling him, you two are just very different and want different things. That's ok too. You do not have to hold on to anyone you don't want to because I don't want you out here playing games with somebody's son. Know that it may not always feel like butterflies and fireworks, but you *do* want to feel special and like the guy you choose adds to your life without all of the doubts and insecurities.

If he feels like your son get out of it. That mother son relationship may be what connects you two, but then resentment will come. You will get frustrated that you carry most of the weight whether its chores, children, bills, working, shopping, etc. He gets complacent and will gain resentment that you are treating him as a child (even though he may act like one). Your boyfriend should be actively working toward his career and business, nit dreaming only. He should have a license and a car if he is of age. The car may not be as mandatory in large busy cities, but think about how you will transport groceries and those babies one day. He should have a job, a means, and a want to provide. This guy should take you on dates and also offer to pay. He should open doors for you; this includes cars as well as building doors. He should have the ability to listen to you speak and show understanding. He should also have the ability to participate in a conversation so that you may learn a lot about him as well.

The guy for you should not want to see you struggle and offer to help when able. You are a Queen my dear, so it's star treatment for you only. No, you are not asking for too much. Many of these guys just got super lazy and we (females as a whole) let them, by being too easy, loose, and too accepting of whatever. There are even women proposing to men.... That is tacky. You better not! The man is the hunter. Let him do his job or someone else can. Sure there are other girls and women who will settle for his lack of commitment, his one text a week and a booty call, but that's not for you. Let her have him if that's what he is all about. I know that we like to look at guys potential. I've been there and his current reality is what matters more. This is because some people are talkers and not doers, which means that there is also a possibility that he may not meet your future expectations. You don't want to end up in that scenario if you have proof early. Also, be sure that you are being a great friend and partner as well. You are the leading lady of this here masterpiece and you are a bonafide star. If not him, there is another gent coming soon to take the co-star role. There is no need to settle for crumbs when gourmet is on the way.

Let's Talk About Sex

I'll begin by saying this: A boy (or man) who cannot cover you in prayer, with love, affection, quality time, and truth, has no business inside of you! A boy without a vision will ruin yours because he doesn't have a plan for you or his future. It

81

will be hard for him to see your vision, even as you elaborate on your great dreams, if he's not there yet. Then unfortunately you get the bad end of the stick intentionally through resentment because he felt pushed into your vision or jealousy because he sees in you what he lacks. He may also cause you unintentional pain because he is plain old lost and frustrated. Either way it's not your fault and not your problem to fix. If he doesn't have a plan in which he is *actively* working toward, walk away and choose not to become a part of his grey area of confusion. I used to think that only wanting a partner with money was shallow and gold digging. If you are working and can pull your weight, but you also want a guy who can bring that plus some, this is not gold digging! That is just smart and more like goal digging. So only date a boy/man who can afford you. Marriage and relationships are like a business. Learn to work smarter, not harder. Women were created to support not to take care of a man. Your job is to stay in character and keep that lead role in your own life. You're going places girl! And you only need to connect closely with other go-getters. He needs to be one as well.

Your virginity and body should be a gift to your marriage, not something given away like an old toy. Those boys, those men, they want the goodies, but make them wait. If you do decide to have sex, at least follow Uncle Steve's advice about the 90-Day Rule. Get to know a guy before having sex with him. Be sure you even like him and you're not just horny. Be sure that he can meet your core needs first and decide if he's worth it. They don't deserve any goodies without treating you with proper respect and commitment to you. I am not saying this as though I waited until I was married to lose my virginity, but I should have. Instead I did what too many young girls do. I gave it up as a teenager on senior prom night in a hotel, I mean motel, but hotel sounds better. He was my boyfriend and sure I was in love.... Yeah right, but I thought so. The bad part is that we called it off not too long afterward and I don't remember the experience as something special. Losing your virginity should be a special experience to remember and not just something on your to do list or as another badge to add to someone's belt.

There are some immature egotistic guys who will slander your name. Now honestly your name can be slandered two ways. The first way is, if you have sex with a guy, be that oral or vaginal he may go around telling his boys, the neighborhood or school. And that's when you may be called easy and a slut. He may go around broadcasting, "I got with her", etc. and you don't want to be that girl. That could be hurtful. The second way a guy will try to slander your name is if you won't give it up or give him the time of day. You may then be called a Bitch, a stuck up girl, and he may even lie telling everyone that he did indeed have sex with you, which means the guy was no good in the first place. Most likely, he would have still spread these messages if you gave him any goods. The good thing about you not giving in is that there is no relevance and you won't feel the shame. It may sting hearing these bad lies about you, but just SMILE really big with confidence because you know the truth. And spread the truth happily saying, "He ain't get none from me and he's mad. Ha ha, ha", "I'm too good for you homey so keep talking". This actually happened to me as a teenager and it was hilarious. He was the mad one. It is better to walk away with your dignity intact and without regret. Because once it's gone, you can never get your virginity back.

When it comes to losing your virginity, it is painful because your hymen, the protective barrier, breaks and you may even see some blood. This pain is bearable and most can get over it quickly, but there is an emotional pain that may come with the rejection of a boy or man after you have sex with them. So choose sexual partners wisely. Many if not most boys are chasing girls due to lust and just want sex, not love. This is due to immaturity, society, and upbringing. Be sure he treats you well, date for at least 90 days before sex, and use protection. Losing your virginity should be sacred and saved for marriage, but unfortunately this is very rare these days. At least make him put in extra effort to indulge in this experience with you. I'm talking rose petals, teddy bears, jewelry, your favorite color everything, his listening ears, positive vibes, and of course those 90 days that gave you confirmation that it may be a good idea.

To avoid getting pregnant, you want to be sure to begin birth control when you think you are ready for sex. Visit a gynecologist to find out which one works for you and be sure to stay on schedule. The pills to me are great and very effective, but they are effective as long as they are used daily and at the same time. If you choose the pill, set yourself an alarm to take it daily child, preferably first thing in the morning so that you are set for the day. For every other option stay in touch with your doctor and keep your appointments. This does not protect against Sexually Transmitted Diseases and Infections (STD's and STI's) when you are sexually active. Some of these diseases are curable, some are treatable, and some can be life long (and life threatening). Contrary to what some believe, the life stealer HIV (Human Immunodeficiency Syndrome) is not a thing of the past. So just to be sure make him wrap it up.

There are many males who may try to pressure you to have sex. Our vaginas were made to make their penises feel good. This is just honestly speaking. Their goal is to get that fix and usually as often and with as many as possible. Some of you are thinking that they won't talk to you anymore if you don't pleasure them. And maybe a guy may even say this to you, but who says he will keep talking to you if you do pleasure him? Then there are others of you who are following friends and feeling like you have to be involved sexually to be a woman, to fit in, and to have something to talk about with your fast tail friends. First of all, it would be best to get rid of those friends who have nothing else to talk about other than sex. Tell them to get some goals! Secondly, if they are really good friends, they should respect your views as well.

Sex should be with someone you share an equal emotional bond with and really you should also be married. There are many emotional pitfalls that can come along with having sex. Many girls believe sex will keep a guy or create a relationship, when in reality to guys sex is usually just that, sex and nothing more. I'm not sure if most girls even enjoy sex. I didn't when I was younger. I didn't even know what I was doing, lol. I think many girls just want to feel desired and are seeking attention, therefore will have sex just to please a guy. Decide that this is not your attention. Be careful and very decisive even over the people you kiss. Hell, I'm still paying for a kissing a boy and catching a disease called mono, as a teenager from a knuckleheaded boy. I have to get my tonsils out because they are inflamed and it began back then. Who knew it would remain a problem? Girl, be decisive and selective.

Instead of having sex like the media and others in society may be pushing, you can choose abstinence. Abstinence is the self-made decision not to indulge in activities that may be viewed as pleasurable. In this instance we are speaking of abstaining from sex and remaining a virgin until you are married or have gotten to know someone who treats you like royalty. If you have already chosen to be sexually involved it does not make you a dirty or horrible person. It is morally wrong to have sex before marriage, but in this world it is almost normal. Don't feel bad or beat yourself up. What you can do now is choose to be celibate. Celibacy is choosing not to engage in sex after you have already lost your virginity and have been sexually active. This says to yourself and others "I am honoring my temple again. I am respecting my temple and to be in relationship with me means you will to." It is difficult for many of us to live up to the standard of waiting until marriage, but it is possible. You can do this girl!

If you are thinking about it, it's time to evaluate your motives and discuss protection from pregnancy, STD's, and STI's. If your motives are keeping a guy, impressing someone or any types of peer pressure it is definitely the wrong motive. Those who are already sexually active you need to question whether or not you want to continue that path and know why. Once again you cannot ever get your virginity back, but you can make a promise to yourself and the Higher Power you believe in to remain true to you and be celibate until you are happily married. You can be a born again virgin. At least that's what I called myself at one point.

If and when you do decide to have sex my strong recommendation is to get tested and ensure that your partner is tested as well. Go together if possible and check the paperwork. His words are not enough. As my Aunt Velma always told be " They lying!" It should be on letterhead from the Doctor's Office or Clinic. If he refuses, honey you should refuse your body as well. There are too many diseases going around nowadays for that nonsense. The highest risk is HIV/AIDS, but there are many other potentially dangerous ones such as Chlamydia, Syphilis, Gonorrhea, herpes, HPV and many more, and I was not sure how dangerous trichomoniasis could be until this girl I knew through someone gave birth to a baby who died because she was carrying this particular disease. The progressive form of HPV can cause cancer if not caught and treated in time. The other diseases can cause the mildest things of bumps, sore throats, and discharge to the worst things of infertility, blindness and even death if not treated properly. I am not trying to scare you. I am telling you to inform you.

It is my belief that females are the most powerful creatures put on this earth if we use our powers for good. Our intuition, our ability to create and our vaginas are super powers. We can get most men to do almost anything for us if we learn the right techniques. Young girls and women your power is beyond belief! I want for you to be unshakeable and it starts with knowing you, loving you, and making good choices for you. Now is the time to learn more about yourself and protect God's temple, which is your body. It's never too late and never too early to protect the goods God has given you.

1. Do you plan to wait until you are married to have sex (again)? Why or Why not?

2. Do you want children? Why or why not? If you do want children, around what age do you want them?

3. What does your ideal mate look like? How does he treat you?

4. Are you dating someone right now? If yes, how do you feel when around him? If no, be patient, be prayerful, and stay on purpose. He will find you.

5. What are ways you can guard your body, your mind, your heart, and your reputation?

Chapter 10
To Be or Not to Be A Role Model

Chapter 10
To Be or Not to Be A Role Model

People who choose to take the stage are role models whether that was their goal or not. This can be a stage play, a real movie, a management position at a company, being a parent, a teacher, and countless other roles. Being alive and really living already puts you in a position to be a role model to somebody. You never know who's watching or whom you may inspire. When people decide to take leadership seriously and lead positively it is a beautiful thing. Unfortunately though, there are many people in the spotlight who do not take their role or platform seriously. Well they take it seriously and become successful, but they don't think about the lives they are impacting. We can no longer just blame the fellas. We have female rappers, singers, actresses, and other influencer's half naked everyday knowing how large their platform is and how many impressionable young girls see and hear them.

I do agree that censorship is partially up to parents. We have to be careful and watchful as to what our children take in and do our best to put locks on what we don't want them to be exposed to yet. The thing is these children have friends, they go to school, have other relatives, and they have YouTube. Right? You cannot protect against everything, but we must do our best. See when I was younger it was much easier. All of the sex-related and violent content was only played on the radio and TV after 10pm when the children were asleep. You could put a lock on certain sites and know that children were even safe on electronics. Now, you can do all of this, but with all of the ads, pop ups, music, commercials and more they can still possibly be exposed to some things that you would rather keep them from. We should still do our parts with locks, parental control, and watch what we play around them, but most importantly we need to talk to our children. Then walk the talk. And young girls you need to talk to your parents. Ask questions. The only dumb question is the one not asked.

Speaking of parents, let's discuss the role of motherhood. There is nothing like accepting your role as role model when you become a mother. You are or will be those children's provider, protector, and example. If it is a young girl, she will mimic you. If you would not be happy with her acting the way you are, work toward change. If you do not like her attitude or behavior, then chances are you have to work on your own change. Who else is she getting it from? Sure there are other influencers, but you as a parent are number one. With you directing your life positively and you doing your best in that role, you will get there. If you don't have children yet, you will remember these words one day when you need them. Another thing to accept is that your parents are not perfect, so forgive them. Chances are they did and do their best with the tools and knowledge they have. Nobody enjoys being miserable and not doing their best, but sometimes we get stuck. To change, people have to realize the error, learn a new way, and practice the new technique. It takes time when you do try to change. It's not easy, but it's possible for everyone willing to try and put in full effort.

With this, let's talk a bit about forgiveness. Forgiveness is not forgetting or pretending that someone did not hurt us. Forgiveness means to let go of the power it has over us. Forgiveness is accepting people, as they are, whether we choose to stay connected or not. Forgiveness is saying, 'Yes, that hurt me, but I know that what you did or said is a reflection of you and not me.' People act and speak based off of their mental maturity and capacity. You don't know what your parents or any other human had to endure to be himself or herself so try not to judge yourself based off of them. Hopefully they are great role models who can be good guides. Parents are like super heroes, but we do have to remember that they are very human. Only God can really judge you as well as them. Only God knows all about your past and your future. You have your parents DNA, but honey they are not your Maker. The Amazing Creator of the Universe created you and you are perfect for your purpose.

Lord knows I have had moments of impatience, I have said a few things I regret, and I don't always feel like the perfect parent, but I do my best. I know that I always mean well and I think they know too. That's what matters. Most times I do more for them than I do for myself or at least before myself because that is what a mother should do. I know that my children are well taken care of, they feel my love and my support, and so I have to be kinder to myself. I suggest you do the same. This is in the case that you are doing your best. Don't give yourself permission to continue to mess up or not reach the goals you set as a role model and caretaker. But do learn from the mistakes and create a strategy to deal with situations better in the future. We all must practice patience and kindness in all things. Those are indicators of love.

There is no parenting manual so we all fall short and we will all make mistakes. Pray, cry, smile, praise and keep pushing through. The great thing about children is that they forgive and will love you through it. This is not an excuse not to change though, it is just assurance, because we can still scar our children. Our children deserve the best treatment as well as a great or at least decent role model. Teach them to love themselves by loving and respecting you, then in turn loving, respecting, and being patient with them. If you have children remember that if you want change in any area, you must first be the change. Humans, including our children, are more influenced by what we do than what we say, so that is why I say *Be* the change. In most instances, your children will naturally follow. Even if you don't see it now, you are planting seeds and those seeds will grow in and through them. Then in some ways your children will always and forever be different than you because they have a different purpose. As a parent it is up to us to learn to accept them for who they are. Your children came here with their own role to fulfill in their movie. They have genes from their father and your ancestors, plus their purpose may require different from their First and more influential Father or Creator, God. You have to learn to accept and respect that, but keep doing your best.

For those who don't have children, continue to be strong and stand in your abstinence or celibacy, most boys are not worth it. If you are sexually active, continue to use condoms and birth control as protection (remember, set that alarm if needed). If you know you don't want children right now, no matter how good it feels or who has to go to the store, condoms first. Matter of fact; be prepared yourself when you know that sex is a possibility. I do believe that sexually active girls and women should carry condoms. Some think that it is a guy's responsibility. Well it is great if he has it, but it is not his job alone. Honestly, many guys would rather no condom anyways and hope that you'll be fine with it. Another thing is there are some folks who poke holes in condoms to pass STD's or to cause pregnancy, so don't rely on him. Tell him wrong one! Matter of fact show him and pull out your own protection ladies! Any type of condom is fine, but try to carry at least one Trojan because all guys think they need the larger condom, lol. It does something for their ego, so hey.

Even with all of the protection, when you engage in sex, unplanned things can still happen. A condom breaks, a condom falls off, a condom comes off inside of you, or you forego it altogether (telling yourself, just this once). After orgasm or at least after someone cums the tingling rubs off and you are like *Oh snap!* What about disease? What about pregnancy? What about my promise to myself? The first thing you do is get to a drug store and pick up a Plan B pill. You may even be able to get one prescribed from your OBGYN for emergency situations, as this, so that you can get to it sooner. Plan B is an emergency form of contraceptive. It is a one-time pill that one can take to stop a pregnancy before it starts. This is not something that you want to take often. It is filled with hormones, which our body already has and therefore has side effects. It is for emergency only. Plan B does not protect against any STD's or STI's, so do your best to protect yourself. Nothing, but abstinence is 100% and will guarantee that you won't get a disease, infection, or pregnant. If you do become pregnant and that is not a part of your plan, you then have some very tough choices to make. Do you go on to prepare for motherhood? Do you keep the baby and put the baby up for adoption? Or do you terminate the pregnancy with abortion? I know these are tough questions, but these are your real life choices.

Trust me, I know. I have had abortions. Yes plural, more than one. This is not easy, but I have to put myself out there. I had to let someone know that you are not alone in this world with these decisions. I am not the only one, if you've been through this, you are not the only one. You are still a good person if you have chosen abortion. If you are feeling guilt, pray about it and know that you are forgiven. I am hopeful that with proper education and guidance that we can lower the abortion numbers. I wasn't even fast, so don't think that only loose fast tail girls get pregnant. No one is immune and don't judge others. I lost my virginity at 18 and I've slept with less than two handfuls of guys in my life. Only two were ever unprotected and all of my pregnancies were by the same person, even the mistakes. When I had the first abortion, I was young and missing birth control pills. This is why I highly recommend an alarm. And when I say to you, I've had a few abortions and only one was because I decided not to use protection, it's the truth. The others were from condoms falling off and sliding so far up inside me that I could barely reach it. Those bloopers happen people!

I regret not being more responsible with my birth control, and then I would not have had to experience this. I am completely Pro-Choice, but I do believe we need to do our best to protect ourselves. An abortion is a surgery, so we are putting our bodies through it. When we are given pain medication and being put to sleep, who knows what that really does to your body? I don't. I'm not really trying to find out. I've prayed on it and never want to go through it again, that's all I know. I do not recommend abortions, they are painful, it can be an emotional roller coaster, and most importantly it is not birth control. So protect yourself young lady. Although it may clean up your mess, it is not the easiest choice and may not be the best way to go.

If you already have children or want children, remember that children are a Blessing. Babies are beautiful inside and out, but it takes a lot to raise a child right. It takes time, money, patience, and the sacrifice of your individual goals and dreams. You can definitely still achieve any goal you set; it may just take longer to reach because you have to first make sure those kids are all set. On the other side, having children will make you step it up a bit. When you know that you have to provide and that they are watching you, something in you will go harder. Having children to feed can definitely be a motivator. If the only person dependent upon you is you, I'm encouraging that until you are ready to provide for others as well. This means providing money, time, education, and resources for those children to grow and thrive. Get yourself in order and take care of you first, so that when you have children you can focus your attention on them, instead of trying to raise you both.

Having children is amazing. Being a mother is one of the best roles in the world. I would not trade it for a thing. My girls are the best, they rock! You, young lady rock! So your children will rock! I don't always know what I'm doing, but I do my best. What I am learning to do is to ask for help. I had a hard time with this, feeling as that I should know and have it all together. This is especially true for me because my mother is not around and to me, Grandma is the only sure person, happy to spend time with her grandbabies very often. My children and I don't have that and we don't quite have a nanny yet, so I really had to learn to ask for a hand because we have to take care of ourselves as well ladies. You are not superwoman so ask for help. It is ok and a sign that you understand your needs, not weakness. It takes a village. You want the right village, but it does take one. We are not perfect and no one has the ultimate parenting handbook. These children are watching and we are their guide.

In my opinion the root of many of our issues begin at home because that is where the teaching and learning starts. So we have to work on ourselves to provide not just financially, but to provide great role models for the next generation. I want to add that, whether your parents are involved or not, every individual is responsible for making their own decisions to impact their future. You are not your parents. Their mistakes are theirs; their successes are theirs as well. It is time to be your own person and that means you need to get to know you, accept you, love you, and be transparent about you. You rock girl!

1. Who is your role model or greatest influence? Why?

2. How are you currently being a role model for others? Are you having a negative or positive impact? Why?

3. How did your parents do well raising you? Where did they totally screw up? What could they have done better? Have you forgiven them for their shortcomings?

4. As a mother or mentor what do you do well to impact those children? What areas can you use improvement? What strategies will you use to make those improvements?

5. If you want to be a mother some day, or they are really young, how can you prepare now to be the best example and influence for your child(ren)?

Chapter 11
The Climax

Chapter 11
The Climax

A movie gets real good with chaos. I mean, right as things are going smoothly, something crazy occurs to make things interesting and confusing. You will also have a climax, or 3, or 4 in real life! The conflict may be a bad break up, an unplanned pregnancy, loss of income, a friend or relative not being who you thought they were, your health is threatened, someone close to you dying, or another issue. You know you hit a climax because your world seems to be turned upside down. You may be moody, feel depressed, you may be angry and not know why. Something occurred. When you meet people that act these ways, remember not to take it personal, something happened. The good thing about a climax though is that it is a turning point. A turning point forces change. Yes, change is scary because it's different, but change is necessary and the only thing consistent throughout life. Knowing that change is a constant, it is then up to us to decide how we will respond to change in our lives.

Who would've thought that it would take my blood pressure going up so far that I feared for my life, being homeless, and losing my car, for me to step all the way up? I wouldn't have. My plan was to grow up, have an amazing career, be happily married, travel, have a few children, travel some more, and not have a real worry or care. And this was all by age 27, I thought. I had big plans ya'll! Shoot! I have two degrees! I never thought I would worry about bills or think twice about my health being jeopardized this young. I sure did have a wake up call or three because life happens to us all.

I am the furthest thing from lazy and I am always busy, so it's not laziness. I've always worked. The only times I seemed to lose jobs were when I was pregnant and had no full control on grabbing another job quickly. Check this! In October of 2009 during my first pregnancy, I was let go from my job at a nonprofit. And in November of 2014 I was laid off from my bank job. I thought this was super crazy and a form of discrimination because I was pregnant. I did file a suit against the nonprofit in 2009, but I decided to drop it and let God handle it. I didn't need the stress. With the bank job on the other hand, they covered well because they laid off a few other people from different branches in the same position. They were strategic about theirs, so I let that go too. Both times I chose to focus on what was baking in the oven as I collected unemployment and planned for the future.

What I learned looking at both scenarios is that there had to be a reason. I didn't quit and I wasn't a bad employee. In fact, I had a good job in between these two in which my boss did not want to let me go. I think the reality is that God wanted me to rest during these times. He may have been protecting my babies and myself. And not just that, He knew better than I did that I was settling. Neither of those positions were paying me my worth and they were not fully aligned with my purpose. God was pushing me into discomfort so that I had to seek purpose. The pain came to give me purpose. If I did not reach my breaking point I would not be as passionate as I am now. It took for me to be broken to realize my place in all of this mess. Most bad things that happen in our lives are not directly our faults, but if we are honest, we may have to take some ownership. Now, I did not do anything crazy to be let go from either job, but being honest with myself I had it coming because I was settling. I wasn't playing full out because those jobs weren't really meant for me. I was good at them perhaps, but my purpose is so much bigger than those positions. For my Bachelor's I majored in Mass Media Communications, but neither job was that. As you now know I have big dreams to touch lives and help thousands and millions of women. Those jobs could have possibly financed the mission, but they would not have led me to them.

So I had to look at my life and analyze it. Why was I settling? When did the settling begin? Something happened. Some of it was before I had children, so I can't say that it was because I had to feed, cloth, and house my girls. Looking back, I had been settling for a while, but I was comfortable with it. For one, I did not realize it and two, when you are a teenager and in your 20's you think you have forever to get things together. You do have time young ladies, so don't rush, but pray on your decisions and try to live within your calling as often as possible. There are young millionaires and business owners, so it is never too early! We all may settle at some points, just trying to pay bills, buy things we like, to keep up with the Joneses, and we may at times walk in the path that society sets for us. My hope for you is that you will jump toward all of your goals through prayer and calculated risks. Settling is ok if you don't want more out of life, but if you do and try to ignore the call you will only hurt yourself. Are you settling in your career, at work, in your relationship, or friendships?

For me, I realize this settling and undoing of myself started many moons ago. I believe it began in childhood. Like we discussed before, in my family we were given no real voice or choice so I learned to go along to get along. Also, I was not raised, living with my mother or father since the age of 5. I had no say in that and I am sure that took a toll on me. I am grateful that my mother was able to raise me until age 5, because those are critical developmental years, but we need our mothers always if we have a choice, right? My father and I have a solid foundation now, but we did not live in the same home as I grew up, so we did not have a great emotional bond. My Dad always made sure that I had what I needed and I am grateful for that. I am grateful for our relationship and talks now. So although I felt every bit of undoing as a young 30 year old, I believe I fell apart much earlier.

It could have been at age 5 when my mother was hospitalized and never came back home to live with me. When this first happened, I'm sure a part of me went away too. At times I even felt embarrassed because my mother was the only one I knew that needed a wheelchair and could not do for herself. I held on and stayed positive through the power of hope. And let's not forget prayer because our mother taught us to pray. Or maybe it was at age 14 when my mother passed away. At this point I had given up hope of living together again. I was disappointed, afraid, and felt excluded. Just last year I went through the motions, asking myself "What was it like for you Christina?" Looking at my young children, I can't imagine what losing me would be like for them. Moms are like *Everything!* They'd be devastated, but I know they'd get through it. The thing is I know they'd get through, because I did. I taught and equipped them with everything I knew, everything I've learned, and everything they could ever be, which is anything! I did not give them perfection or competition, but I taught those girls about faith, believing in themselves, and how to pray. May they never forget it. I am really still not fully certain on exactly when my undoing occurred, but I do know there is some relation of my adult chaos to my childhood. I'm just out here with God piecing it back together.

I used to be a Visitation Specialist through DCF (Department of Children and Families) and that was one of the hardest jobs of my life. It took such an emotional toll on me, but the families trusted me and many opened up to me. Maybe they could sense my true understanding. The toughest part is when children would cry after a visit and it was time to go back to their foster homes. I'll tell one story in particular. There was a 6-year-old girl bawling in the car as we drove and I could not just keep silent when I knew that pain. I said, "I know it's hard, but it will be ok." She went on to cry and asked "Why am I crying, but my baby sister is not?" I explained to this young girl, "Your sister is just about to be two years old and does not have the connection and as many memories with your parents as you do. Plus she has you. You're her big sister, so she still has comfort." She seemed to pause crying and nodded a bit as though she understood, but the tears continued to flow. This was okay, but I believe I was placed in that position to help those children so I added,

"Hopefully you will be living with your mother again soon, but either way, one day you will feel better. I grew up without my mother so I understand what you are going through, but you will be ok."

See, I knew this pain far too well, because although I lived with family, I still visited my mother in the hospital and had to leave countless times. Most people are at least raised by their mothers even if daddy is absent, so it was rough on my sister and I. I know that we are not alone. So if you have felt abandoned due to death, neglect, hospitalization, or for any other reason, I want to tell you the same thing I told that young girl. The pain you feel is real. It hurts, but embrace it. It is not meant to break you without rebuilding you stronger and wiser. You will learn so much about yourself and others. Every lesson you learn is meant to be passed on to your family, community, and the tribe you are meant to serve.

We go through so much, even as children and then it impacts our future as adults. I'm no exception. I lived with my aunts and grandmother until I completed college, got a job and had my first child. I am forever grateful that my family took me in and that I did not go through the state system. I am thankful that I have mainly pleasant experiences growing up. What impacted me most was that my cousins had their mothers and I did not, especially around the Holidays. Thank God for a lot of cousins though because they kept me a bit distracted and preoccupied. We were always having fun and into something.

I didn't realize that my tolerance for pain was so high! Most times we don't realize it until we are faced with a trauma and problem as adults and realize that the issue has deeper roots. I was so used to pain that I knew how to mask it, barely deal with it, and everyone else would think everything is peachy. Not many knew that I struggled emotionally, physically, or financially, until life broke down. Even then, not many knew too many details. Either they didn't ask, I didn't tell, or I looked so put together they assumed that all was mainly fine. Man can we put on a face!

Although I've always tried not to judge others, I would notice struggle and think, 'that won't be me.' But guess what? I did go through struggle. I've also studied people who have made it to where I want to go and you know what I'm learning, all of them have been through struggles too. That's how I know that no one is exempt. We have to stop looking at life as though to be successful means not to struggle. Success means not giving up and overcoming all of the obstacles that get in our way, causing struggle. Sure success looks cute and glamorous on television and on social media, but that's because it's the aftermath. We don't see that dirt rock mountain they had to climb first. Nor do we see their horrible moments, days and dirty laundry, unless it catches the news. They are real people like us. They face opposition, pain, and have the same 24 hours we do. All of us are equally talented and creative, just in different ways. Appreciate your difference. The only thing a millionaire has different than you is money, and you can get that too. The question is how? When you have less money to spend, you must spend your time wisely. Time is our most precious commodity with or without money because we can't get an hour, minute, or second back. So value and protect your time! God is on your side, but everyone gets the same amount of time to choose what they will do.

As you are going through life setting and reaching goals, the climaxes in your life will sometimes look like failure and defeat. It is only failure though if you give up on yourself or on life. Look at failure as slipping and falling. Therefore you have the option to get up and try it again. It is a choice. Falling can be painful and you may get a little bruised, but it is something about falling that is great. We learn the best lessons from failure, falling, and our setbacks. Falling, but not dying helped me to see that God has me and is here to help me. Falling hard helped me to gain a new boldness and thirst for life. I am still an introvert, but I can assert myself better, I can speak in a room full of people now. I may still have the urge to shrink, but I am able to stand tall through it now. Showing up will bring you opportunities. Because I decided to use my voice to help and encourage others I am a #1 Best Selling Author, recognized Nationally and Internationally. I was asked (by Holly Porter herself) to be a part of the collaborative book *30/30 Rules: What I Wish I Knew in My 20's,* all because I decided to use social media as a vehicle to uplift others. Some may say it is just a coincidence, but I am sure it was a part of the divine plan. I was already writing this book when we connected. Being a #1 Best Seller helped my platform by giving me a new title and it's a great launching pad for the rest of my career and business decisions.

In this life you will get knocked down. You will get your feelings hurt and you will be abandoned. Know that. You will most likely be betrayed, lied to, and lied on. Remember the fact that hurt people hurt other people and everyone hurts at some point. So when people are insensitive, say mean things, try to hurt you physically, or are dishonest with you this has been done to them. In their head this is how the world works and they may target you because you look too content for their reality. Misery loves company. Do not feed into it though. Do report what you need to, defend yourself, and then keep your distance from these types of people. They want to still your joy, but you deserve happiness no matter what, so they can't have it! Right?! So, when you get knocked down due to your mistakes or the wrongdoings of others, the key is to always get back up. You were made for this! You are a champ and this role was made for you.

Because we are on a journey in which we are meant to continuously learn, you will encounter multiple difficult situations. Once you make it through that first difficult time, you will gain strength and confidence to make it through the rest. Each time will hurt, but with the perspective of "I got through it before" the struggles will be easier. You will not be immune to the pain, but you will know that you can make it through. Sometimes we also have to stop relying on ourselves too and lean on a Higher Power. We are unable to do everything ourselves. There is an opposing force that is going to do it's best to make it difficult trying to get you to give up, to settle and not go forward toward your dreams and purpose. The greater your calling the harder the fight, but you can be well equipped with faith, a plan, and action. Once you decide to press forward and break through that barrier you will break forth to the next level and see that it is well worth it.

You are working on a great one and the truth is, all great movies have serious conflict. All conquerors and successful beings chose to overcome them. This includes you, so choose faith over fear. Sometimes we have to accept that conflict is a part of our life movie, just to make it great! When conflict comes, you know things are really going to turn around. Devon Franklin said it best, "The greater the villain, the greater the hero!" So yeah it may be tough at times, but my dear you are tougher! Those who are knocked down the lowest have the ability to spring back up the highest. So get ready to leap!

1. Have you recently experienced a climax or turning point in your life? If so, what is it and where is it directing you?

2. What are you battling right now that you just can't seem to shake? Have you prayed on it? Have you talked about it to a trusted counselor, relative, or friend? Why or why not?

3. What is your earliest memory of conflict or trauma? How did that impact you?

4. What is something that you went through before and never thought you could live through it, but you did? Celebrate!

5. Write 3-7 things you are grateful for and why.

Chapter 12
Cut! Take Care of Yourself

Ch. 12
Cut! And Take care of yourself

To keep our attention, movies, shows, and even commercials nowadays have to contain humor and/or some type of suspense. Some of it is just pure ridiculousness. Have you noticed? I mean, you can watch an entire commercial and not be fully sure what the product is until the end. There's a car, an animal, soda, and a sports figure in the same 30-second ad these days. Does it really take all of that? With all that we ingest maybe it does, because it peaks interest. What I do know is that life and information are coming at us quickly and we have to be sure to take moments to slow down and chill out from time to time. You want to get everything done, keep your passion and fuel, without risking burn out.

It's about creating a balance. This is tough when you have a family I know. For example, I have a hard time letting my children walk around looking ashy and hair a hot mess, while I'm looking like a million bucks. Therefore, there have been times I am unable to do my own hair. I just throw on a wig, gel those edges and keep it moving, but that's not ideal. I will never let my children walk around looking like complete ragdolls, but I have decided that mommy will take the time to do her hair or get it done more often. Even if it means their hairstyles have to stretch a few more days or a week, because mama needs to look and feel good too. Balance means taking turns. It is not easy, but it can be done. We must choose to use our time more wisely. We can all look good and take care of ourselves. We are their example after all. I've heard of women being hospitalized over dehydration, but the people they care for are flourishing. Crazy right? Doing for ourselves last? It's time to break free of this cycle. Put you as a priority on your list girl! I know I've bumped me up. If we aren't healthy it will be hard to take care of anyone else, so bumped up to number one priority is a must. This does not give us permission to neglect our responsibilities or the people important to us. It just shows them and ourselves that we matter too. A healthy dose of self-love is what we all deserve.

Be sure to protect your mental health ladies! Start with asking questions when they arise. There is no such thing as a dumb question, other than the question not asked. Chances are, if you have a question, others have it too. Most are just not brave enough to speak out. Go be that brave one. I don't know what it was with me when I was younger, but I had a hard time asking questions and I thought I should know it all. I guess I still battle with this a bit because I've had to unlearn it, but I'm more comfortable now. Nobody knows it all! We become wiser with knowledge and seeking answers to questions is the best way to do learn more. Also, be ok with seeking counseling when difficult problems and decisions arise. Pray about it all for sure, but it is also a good idea to find a licensed therapist that you trust to help walk you through tough issues. The other thing you want to do to help yourself is to ask for help. Man, we have to put that cape on the hook more often! You will need help at school, at work, help raising children, help in relationships, help in business, and more. Get okay with this! We are not superwoman! Not any of us. Sure, we could do it all and figure it all out alone, but chances are it would not be at our best. Show me a person who was made 100% perfect in every area then I'll believe different. I'll wait, because they don't exist. If they appear to have it all together though, and often, then they put on that mask we all wear as superwoman or they have a village of helpers. We all need help. It took me some time to accept this, but I'm building my team of help and I am also helping others along the way. Seek help and lend a hand. That's what I believe in. We are in this together because we are stronger together.

If we are going to discuss our health, let's also talk about body image and weight. You don't need to be a size 2 or a size 6. If you are a smaller size and healthy and it works for you, great! If not, that is pretty great too! Because we are all made in different forms. Healthy comes in all sizes. Some people would be very unhealthy at size 6 or under, so you have to know you. The biggest thing is that you are healthy. Although we don't want to strive to be a size, we also want to be mindful of our body's signals. If you feel sluggish, are diagnosed with diabetes, high blood pressure, high cholesterol or any other health related issue, it is important to take care of yourself. Be sure to exercise, eat proper nutrition, get proper rest, and maybe lose a few pounds if it can help. Let us strive to feel well and be well instead of temporary wins because there are so many options.

The world is always coming up with quick fixes and easy buttons. I do admit that some conveniences are amazing and make our lives so much easier. There are some things though that shows we are taking the easy way out instead of doing the work. There is a pill and a wrap for everything. You want longer hair? There's a pill for that. You want to lose weight? There are pills for that. You want to take a few inches of weight off? There are wraps, cinchers, waist trainers, and more for that. I'm not sure if any of them work because I have not tried them. It may vary because every body is different. My concern is are the ingredients FDA approved? Are there any long-term side effects to be concerned about? What ingredients are in those items to make them trim certain areas and grow others? I'm a bit concerned so that's why I haven't tried most. What I do for me and what I believe in, is a good workout, eating right, and plenty of water. Exercising for 30-60 minutes everyday can do wonders over time child!

Many girls and women struggle with weight and eating disorders due to not being in love with their bodies. Love your body, every inch of it! No matter how big or how small. Some females battle with anorexia as well as bulimia trying to win a beauty pageant, a modeling contract, or in general trying to look like a person the media tells them is beautiful. For those who do not know what I am referring to, anorexia is when a person maintains an abnormally low body weight due to compulsive exercise and starvation. A girl who is anorexic may think she is fat because she has a distorted body image and she is usually underweight. Bulimia is an eating disorder where a female may binge eat and then force herself to throw up to avoid gaining weight. In both instances, the individual does not love herself as she is. I need you to know darling that you are beautiful as you are. Just be yourself, live the healthiest lifestyle you can and be the light that shows other girls and women they can do it too. These disorders can be just as bad as drugs, because they are habits that are hard to stop and many people need programs and much support to quit. The best way to avoid the aftermath is not to start these habits in the first place. Instead exercise, eat right most times, and communicate with others or at least your journal to get your feelings out.

Then there are those that don't feel they have enough assets-booty and breasts- and they get surgery to make them bigger. Some live by Botox and get their lips, face, and other body parts done too. Baby girl, just remember you are beautiful as you are and God created you with all you need. For some reason if you do desire to get more added to you, by all means do what works for you, just get it done safely. Know your whys, pray on it, and think of all the pros and cons for a while before getting any work done. If the answer is yes, please see a medical Professional in a Professional cosmetic surgery setting. I have heard too many stories of people getting hurt or even dying because they let some unlicensed person add all types of elements to their frame in their backyard somewhere. Oh no, sweetie, don't do it! Check licenses, ask questions, and do background checks. You don't want cement in your face or behind! Most of the time people are comparing themselves to a completely fake image anyways. There are woman who have had tons of work to supposedly look perfect and then their picture is still Photoshopped. By the time we see some images in magazines, they are completely digital creations. Don't compare yourself to some fictional character. That's basically what many media images are, just made up. Don't believe the hype! You are enough, beauty and brains.

Nutrition is so important. You never know how important, something as simple as Fiber is, until your body goes into whack without enough. Being constipated and backed up is not fun. What is worse is your appendix being inflamed and having to be removed due to toxicity and infection-appendicitis they call it. To my girls and all girls of the world, eat your fiber and eat as healthy as you can. Raisins, prunes, and whole grains are your friend. I had my appendix removed at age 23, so I know. Listen to your body and don't ignore urgent signs on any body part. Now, you don't want to go into a frenzy every time your stomach or head aches, please don't, just get in tune with your body and treat it well.

My Director God was looking out for me that time. He always is! I went to one Hospital who told me I had food poisoning and sent me home with a medication. I threw up all types of green stuff. Yuck! It was crazy! But I went home and laid down. That's all I could do, I could barely move around and could not stand up straight. My Grandmother knew something wasn't right so she called one of my aunts and she brought me to Hartford Hospital and they found the real problem. My family may not be perfect, but they did pull it together for that crisis with prayers and presence. This is in my family history, but can happen with or without a family history so your job is to take care of your one body. My body needs extra fiber, yours may need extra vitamin C, D, K, or Iron. Ask questions about your family history to protect your body and take care of you. If your examples don't eat healthy and are battling health issues, you may not want to make those eating choices when you have choice or are able to provide for yourself. Unhealthy can be so much more convenient, but your body will thank you for healthy foods. I read a quote by Russell Simmons recently and it said, "Every time we eat, we are either feeding disease or fighting it."

What?! Think about it. This is powerful and truth. Eat well, live well, and rest well.

We also have to protect our mental health too. For me, this means daily prayer, journaling, taking at least 15 minutes alone, going to Zuumba and yoga each week, and trying to eat right. Between the trauma we may encounter in life and the fact that we are always going, going, going, we have to stop the movie for a minute to take care of self. We are so used to moving, that it becomes hard to slow down, stop, and breath for a moment. Even mediation can be difficult. I want to challenge you to begin taking at least 5 minutes a day to just breath and be. Don't think, don't plan, don't read, none of that. Just breathe and listen to your breath. It will be hard at first I promise, but with time it will get easier. For those of you who were taught that meditation is weird, no its not, lack of knowledge and practice makes it sound weird to some. Ignorance is not always bliss. What meditation is, is connecting with yourself and your Higher Power. When we are doing and moving, we are connected more so to the world. Meditation centers us. Having this moment of quiet can also spark creativity. It's amazing the ideas and vision that have come just from having moments of peace and silence.

Take time to breath and think before acting, especially when stressed and making decisions. Ask yourself why you are bothered? Dig deeper to figure out what is behind it all because it is time to pluck the root! Are there any thoughts or memories that cause you to question your value? Do any particular words, statements, or situations cause you to question if you are good enough? Be honest with yourself because we all have them. The level of impact and the details vary from person to person, but we all share similar feelings. We all feel love, joy, jealousy, resentment, shame, guilt, as well as inadequacy. It's what we do when we feel those ways that matter. When you are angry or feeling less than do you lash out, go into silent mode, or try to sabotage others? Those may not be the best ways to deal. Instead pluck through reasons why you have the negative feeling and turn it into a positive. For example, if a friend got a new job, received good grades, won a prize, or has a new boyfriend, instead of feeling jealous, turn it into joy. Be happy for them knowing that yours is coming at the right time.

As we discussed before, there are some folks we have to let go of, if they cause us to feel bad about ourselves. Put up your not allowed sign! Once you deal with a person and they cause stress or grief you have to decide for yourself if they deserve another chance to get close to you. They may cause the pain again. And worse, you may lose trust in yourself for deciding to give them another chance. So use caution with people. You're amazing so you want to feel good about yourself at all times. No person should come between that. When our judgment is off about a person or situation it can cause confusion and we forget how to trust ourselves. You have to practice forgiveness with yourself. Sometimes we are the hardest people to forgive because we believe it's our job to protect ourselves. Let the person or thing go because you have to get select amnesia with these types of things and forgive yourself. Besides God's your Protector and He has your back! We all deal with guilt and shame because we could have done and said better, but it's time to learn from it and move on. If you are really having a hard time coping with your decisions turn to a trusted relative, friend, or mentor, and strengthen your prayer life with your Director. You have to love yourself through your mistakes. It is a part of the beauty of you. Love that you have flaws and beauty. Accept yourself for both and respect that you are wonderfully made.

When it comes to respecting ourselves, it's important that we discuss dating, break ups, and ending other relationships. Get to know you and love you before trying to love anyone else. They will treat you as you treat yourself. When you respect yourself and boundaries, others have no choice but to follow suit or disappear. Some will walk away because they don't understand your power or level of respect. Then there are others who will still choose to cross boundaries or be disrespectful. You have no authority to stop them. Your power is in what you do with it. At the point of disrespect that person needs to be repositioned in your life. You can choose to either demote them or remove them, depending on the severity of offense. Show people how to treat you by taking care of you and respecting yourself and your boundaries. This will lead to loss of relationships and break ups. This is never easy and is easier said than done. I never thought that I would try again with a cheater, I did, and it was a mistake. You have to decide what your boundaries are. Sometimes you don't know until you are in it, but the discomfort will tell you. Listen to your gut and instinct.

When we are hurt by betrayal, unkind words, rejection, we experience heartbreak. Own it. Say I'm hurt. Go ahead and grieve. Denial only keeps us there longer. It will be uncomfortable, but go ahead and experience the grieving process, which is denial, anger, bargaining, depression, and acceptance. Some talk about grief only in the context of death, but grief occurs any time we experience a loss or traumatic change. This means grief may occur when moving, breaking up, or with divorce. So know that it is normal to feel as though you are on an emotional roller coaster. You do want it to stop though, so focus on taking care of yourself. Take the time to recover and process what went right and what went wrong. Decide what you will do different in the future and what will you keep the same. Look at what you've learned. You may not realize it, but when others hurt you, you can choose to earn wisdom. There are certain signs, queues, gut instincts, and energy levels that you can pay better attention to. Instead of not trusting yourself, use it as a guide and tool in making proper decisions in the future.

I want to repeat, make the decision of where to place people in your life. I learned this tough lesson after just going with the flow of people in my life. Have you seen those movies with the love triangles? You know, when the main character is in love with two different people and doesn't know what to do, so they keep playing the game until they are caught or something crazy happens? That was me. All the way caught up. The only thing is I had no commitment to either guy and neither did they to me, fully. I say fully because I sure expected them to be committed although I was confused not knowing which way to turn. And they also both knew about each other. See, I had just broken up with my boyfriend and decided to date again. While being open and dating again, I decided to open up a spot for my ex-boyfriend, before him. See people are exes for a reason and I had a lapse in judgment due to unforgiveness and not taking time to think things through. Still I kept talking to both, dating both, hanging with both, and having sex with both. Over time I had a slip up, no condom, and forgot to take my birth control, oops! And I decided to have unprotected sex, yikes! What do you think happened? Thank God for no STD! I did get pregnant though. It was then that I finally wanted to make a choice. I had to. Smh. In the past I had abortions so I thought about it briefly. I could not do it though. It felt different this time. She was meant to be here, I wanted her. That was one of the best decisions I ever made! I wanted to think that I made a mistake, but when I look at them, I realize I don't know what I'd do without my daughters. God knows I need them and they need me. The smiles they put on my face daily are priceless! So I'd do it all again, just with a better life strategy.

Staying in that relationship did come at the price of my own happiness on some level though. I could not choose the other guy if I wanted to. Most guys aren't happy raising someone else's child. Especially if you became pregnant while they are dating you. I also, did not want to choose being a single parent, so the guy was chosen for me. That is ok though because I had to own that it all began with my choice, or lack thereof. A better choice would have been to sit back, cut communication with both guys, hold on to my goodies, or at least fully protect myself, as I made a decision on what was best for me. Then *maybe* I would have ended up with the same guy, but it would have been a conscious choice. We want to own our lives, right? I share all this messiness because I can't sit up here and try to act perfect. I am human and have made foolish decisions too. My only hope is that I can help my girls and a few others not make the mistakes I did. So young ladies, sit back, breath, analyze, and strategize.

When people walk out of your life, are dishonest or are boundary crossers know that they were here for a season and a reason. The reason was to teach you, so decide to learn and move on. It does suck learning these lessons, especially at a young age, but that just means you can hone your power sooner than some. What I don't want you to do is begin to look at all people or all males are bad, due to past experiences, because that is not true. Most people are innately good. I do think it is a good idea to respect everybody upon meeting them, but let them earn your trust. Sometimes it is not easy to tell upfront who is worthy of your trust or not. So guard your dreams, possessions, and best kept secrets until they prove themselves worthy.

Women are the pillars of our families and communities. So for the sake of the world, it is my dream that we continue to raise strong, confident, and positive leaders for our future. This starts with a healthy knowledge of self. Learn your strengths, weaknesses, when to say it's time to go harder, and when it's time to say enough. You will learn this with time, but some things we know as children. No matter what the people say around you, respect your likes, dislikes, and your own opinion. You may not feel like a champion at every moment, but know deep down that you are. You matter, your voice matters, and your choices matter. Say this out loud three times right now: *I am strong, I am confident, I am worthy, I am beautiful, I make great decisions, and I am healthy!* Yes you are! We don't uplift ourselves enough, but what a great day to start!

What we sometimes have a hard time talking about and accepting is depression. The thing is, all of us, at least most people, go through depression. Hard times, loss, and struggle can cause so much pain and grief. Know that you are not alone when you feel down and out or alone. We don't want to be a bother to others, so we may even seclude ourselves. Well trust me when I say we all have those feelings at times. What is important at those times is gratefulness. Think of everything you are grateful for, write about those things, talk about those things and praise about those things. Practice doing this happy, mad, or sad and it will come naturally. Be grateful for breath, be thankful that you can hear, see, and talk. Be thankful for working limbs and senses. Be grateful for food and a place to rest your head. Be grateful that you made it this far and be grateful for what you know can and will be in your future. Once your brain connects with all that you do have in your corner, your brain can then relax, get out of survival mode and get in touch with other feelings.

There are times I have moments of anxiety and I know it is time to breath, relax, and connect to my source. It seems and feels like the worse time to stop because there is so much to do, but that's he best time. So I pause to connect with my Creator and myself. With children, a husband, a family, job, social media, housework, cooking to do, writing articles, writing this book, and trying to maintain friendships and a network, sometimes it feels like, How? I know I am not the only one. Right? When you feel overwhelmed and anxious, this is another great time to be thankful. Be thankful for all you have, all you are, and all that you can be. See, the enemy doesn't want our stuff; the enemy wants our minds. Try to keep it together and pull it together when you have to. I used to feel like it should be an issue to have anxiety, like people with anxiety are off and something is wrong, but sugar, what I learned is that every body at some points go through moments of anxiety. This is especially true when you want more out of life and are going for it. It is easy to be at peace and content when you don't want for much. Some folks are built different and they like their lots because to them it's not settling. When you want more though baby it comes with a price. You will have a battle in your mind at times because you don't know if or how you will make it. Just keep pushing though because with faith, a plan, and determination, you will get there.

Whatever relaxes you and is for the greater good, indulge when you can. Some ideas are going on a nice walk, standing or sitting in nature, relaxing in a hot bath, yoga, meditating, journaling, drawing, dancing, or traveling. And don't forget your prayers. Whatever works for you, go for it. Don't care two cents about the opinions of others. They should be focused on taking care of themselves not on judging the next person.

I love the woman I am becoming as I am taking care of me. Through self-reflection and personal development I realized that by nature I am a family first type of woman, but I had to learn balance. I had to remember that I was Classy Chrisy before the kids, and before marriage, I was born Christina. Remember this about yourself because sometimes we get too caught up in the roles and assignments given to us. Remember your purpose and your goals. While juggling school, work, volunteering, sports, children, a husband or not, be sure to get in some well needed Me time. It is so important! If you can squeeze in time with your girls occasionally to let loose, that's awesome too.

When I say that I am great! And I am full of purpose! I say it with humbleness and Godfidence. Because when I connect to my God (the source) He fills me with such energy, zest, strength, and wisdom that I know I'm gifted, but I know who gifted me! As girls and women we downplay our skills all of the time! I'm ready to stop that. I am a great writer! I am gorgeous! I'm a great mother and role model! I am a great dancer! I'm such a creative visionary! It's great to be full of yourself. Who else do you want to be full of? I heard Oprah speak on this one day and I was amazed. If we are full then we have more to give. So connect, recharge and then pour out that energy to the world. On this journey do remember to recharge and take care of self so that you have enough to give others. It's never an excuse to be mean or selfish. There is definitely a difference. Nonetheless dear, you are awesome! You should be full of yourself! This is just the beginning for me! And no matter how young or old this can be a fresh start for you.

1. When is the last time you took time to take care of yourself? What did you do? How often do you do this?

2. How do you find work/school/life balance?

3. Do you ever experience disappointment, stress, anxiety and depression? If yes, how do you cope?

4. What are some tough decisions that you have to make in your life right now? Have you taken the time to do so?

5. What are you doing to gain or maintain a healthy body?

6. How do you practice love for yourself?

Chapter 13
The Trailer

Ch. 13
The Trailer

When folks create movies, we don't think about the large budgets they need to get it done. There are staff to be paid, props, wardrobe, and sets to prepare, so there is a lot to account for. That's how life can be. We have these huge visions of what our futures can look like and the things we can do, but those things take money. And not a little money, our visions take tons of money, so we sometimes shy away. We settle in something smaller or let's say, intimate and live in mediocrity. Fear and inadequacy hits us like, 'I don't have the money for this, I'm too young, I'm too old, I don't have enough connections.' We start to doubt if it was really meant for us, or just a good idea passing through.

On top of this in our religious sectors, we are sometimes taught that Christians are to be humble, not proud, and we should not want. This in so many ways can be interpreted as being okay with lack and less than, which means the Christian is supposed to struggle. Well, I disagree. Yes, you should be humble and not conceited or boastful. That's tacky. But, we do need to be bold in our purpose, in order to influence and guide others toward their purpose. I believe that if you are under assignment by the Creator then you have the divine right and duty to make money, create more money, and share it with those in need. We should have the mindset of *spend some, give some, save some*. Spend some- buy yourself something nice and reasonable occasionally, you work hard. Give some- whether it is 10% at church for tithing, donating to your favorite charity, or volunteering your precious time, give what you can. Save some- put money away in an account for a rainy day. You will struggle at times on the journey because no one is exempt, but that is not your place to stay.

No matter what you dream, if you have the vision, it is for you. God waking you up another day is Him financing your dream. He has more in store, but you have to take the first step to show that you truly believe. Your faith is money in your account that is not accessible yet. Keep stepping out on faith and the money and connections will follow suit. You just have to be patient and relentless in your belief. Waiting is not easy. When you have a hunger and are trying your best, it can seem like success and even progress are forever away. Know that if you are praying, believing, and working, it is on the way. See, your Producer has to get the cast in line. Maybe you chose a cast. Some are working out and some are not. Our God knows exactly who and what is needed to propel you forward. He is preparing you mentally and physically as well. You didn't think the pain and hard times were for nothing, did you? Your endurance and faith were being strengthened. And all of the joy, the glimpses, and the vision you see that does not look like your current reality? He's keeping your hope alive. Those people and opportunities are being lined up just right for the time he plans to open the door to release all of it to you.

I know that being patient, especially for long periods isn't easy. You may feel angry, frustrated, or even abandoned, wondering when God will show up. Some of us are just in agony that we are not living the way our soul knows we are supposed to be. I know that I've been there and still battle with frustration because I am not where I want to be just yet. So go ahead and talk to God, question God, and be still long enough to hear from God. That was one of my weaknesses. Oh I can pray, but that whole stillness thing took some time to master. I still have to remind myself to sit and be still at times. So take your time and keep trying. You are a work in progress.

You may wonder 'How do I know when it's God?' You will learn the difference. One thing is that you feel peace about your decisions when it's God. It's those times you have an *aha* moment and you feel the connection somewhere deep within. God is not the author of confusion, so know that confusion is the enemy trying to keep you from moving onward and upward. It's ok though because the battle is already won. Just pray for guidance and clarity.

All you need is a breakthrough and I am sure it is on the way. If you look at the past I'm sure you will see that you have already encountered and overcome a few things to break through. I mean, just being born is a breakthrough- in more ways than one. Shoot! You had to break something to get here! Breakthrough is made up of two powerful words. The first is break and this means that something has to break, this something may even be you. When God breaks you though He will mend you together better than before, but you have to allow Him to. It may mean that you are broke in the form of finances, broken in spirit, or literally with broken bones. You can and will get through it though if you persevere. The next keyword is that you have to go *through*, not around, or under. Going through hurts. Letting yourself feel the pain, the betrayal, the anger, the shame, and the injustice is painful, but powerful. That's where you get your lessons! And your lessons are your Blessings!

It can be hard to step out on faith and into new territory. With time and experience we learn that we can fall and fail. It hurts and it's scary. I get all that. This is why you must connect with and believe that a Higher Power is working on your behalf. Trusting ourselves after some of our missteps can be tough if that's all we have. We definitely should believe in and have confidence in ourselves, but with your Director guiding your steps you know that you cannot fail, well not permanently, because God cannot fail. Sometimes we have to fall a few times as a part of the learning and growing process. Look at babies learning to walk. They gain confidence through tumbling and getting back up to try again. Babies also look at and look to their caregivers to get that boost of confidence, and you must look up and above. God's got you! I do have confidence, but I now like to call it Godfidence. On my own I have been lost, but with my Higher

Power guiding me, I know that I'll be fine. Get you some Godfidence, love.

With this newfound Godfidence you have to know that He is not just watching and guiding, He also lives inside of you. That is why it is so important to listen to that gut feeling and intuition. That's usually your spirit and it knows and senses more than your brain does. When it says move, then move. When it says no, take the no. Once you learn to trust and follow your inner guide, you will be at peace and have the Godfidence to do anything you know is meant for you, trembling and all.

It all starts with believing in yourself and your tribe will believe in you as well. What tribe you ask? You were meant to teach and lead some folks. It may be one human at a time or small groups, workshops, or arenas. Only God knows because we all have different visions and purposes. Your role is to get in tune with yours. You have to accept your pain points to honor your purpose. Most times it's in the pain you make it through that your purpose is being shown to you. How can someone else learn from your story? Go tell that story, live like an overcomer, and find out.

There are plenty of platforms to use. One platform is social media. Some people treat Facebook, Instagram, and Twitter as their personal venting board. I warn you not to do that. It is ok to uplift and inspire through tough things you overcome, but please do not air your dirty laundry online or in public period. What I mean by this is it is not the place to tell everyone about an argument with your best friend or about how horrible your boyfriend is. First of all, most people will wonder why you choose to be with them. Some may like it and feed into it because they enjoy drama, but it's time for us to cut that cord. I understand that it's fun, easy to receive, and give information, but use social media to your advantage. It is a branding board. Also, if you are looking for a job or want to be seen as a Professional, be sure your posts and pictures are appropriate. Hiring managers do check social media to learn all about candidates. Put your best image forward. Also, do not bad mouth your boss, co-workers, or the company you currently work for via social media. People definitely have gotten fired for this type of thing. Use social media to position the way you want the world to see you. You are building a brand because social media showcases your global reputation. That's why most people's lives look so glamorous. We see highlights of what is good. Their bad days, moments, and rough patches are not broadcasted. Do yourself a favor and do the same. No looking messy on social media girl!

When I began to step out on faith, being more vocal and visible, especially on social media, is when I began to gain a following and opportunities. With this, I became a #1 Best Seller, after I was invited to be a part of a book collaboration titled *30/30 Rules: What I Wish I Knew in My 20's*. I also received more opportunities to write and be a part of multiple events. Being transparent about your real life purpose will draw to you the opportunities needed to reach your destiny. For some reason, even through social media, people can feel authenticity and they gravitate toward it. So be you and walk in your purpose!

Social media is tricky though because you don't want to be a completely different person in person. So don't post anything false or crazy, but post the real great parts of you. My social media and brand are very uplifting and encouraging. That is me in real life, and when I am coaching or mentoring. In my close circles though I do have venting sessions, and I tell them why I'm mad. I'm a full human! When people meet me they may expect some outgoing woman ready to preach to everyone. That is so not me. I am a total introvert, until you play some music I like. I love to dance and I will get a party started if I love the music. I am so not a follower, but I also don't always want to lead. So I am real chill and observant. For some reason I used to want to be an extrovert, all outgoing and mingling, but I now love my personality and all of me. I learn a lot being just the way that I am. I am very observant, a great listener, and I pick up on energy like nobody's business. I am a hugger too, so if you feel a connection, I may too, so get ready for an embrace. I don't hug everyone though because my goal is to keep negativity away. It's ok to be choosy. Energy is real and somewhat contagious. I only hug if the energy feels right.

What can also speak loud as energy in this world is your credit score. Those three numbers are so important that that they determine if you are approved for credit cards and loans and at what interest rate. For those who are not familiar, your credit score is a 3-digit number assigned to a person that suggests their probability in repaying debt based off of their credit history. Most credit scores range between 300 to 850, anything at 700 or above are considered good or excellent, 649 and below is considered poor or bad credit, and the numbers in between are considered as fair. To get and maintain good credit the first thing I will tell you to do is pay for most things with cash or debit from your bank account. Once you or your parents decide that you are responsible enough to apply for a credit card be sure to pay all balances on time and preferably in full, but always pay the minimum balance at least. To keep your payment low, purchase low, it is in my opinion a good idea to buy a soda and a pack of gum using your credit card, just to pay it back later that day. To build credit, the amount of the purchase doesn't matter as much as the amount being paid back and on time does. So you don't have to go on a shopping spree or buy big-ticket items to build credit.

I would stress staying away from credit all together, because it can cause so many problems, but the reality is you will most likely need credit one day. I am no credit or financial guru, but when I decided to get a loan for my first car, I went to three different banks before I was approved because of my lack of a credit history. If you do not find a bank to approve your loan application, you may need a Co-signer and not everyone will sign off on the promise to pay when it is not for them. I knew for me, that was a long shot option, so I was excited when I was finally approved! Even if you do have someone who will help, you do want to be independent, so build your credit and be sure not to abuse it. Credit can also impact other areas of your life, such as your career, so you want to take care of it. You can literally miss out on a new job or promotion because your credit score is not viewed as worthy and responsible enough to handle it. How rough is that? It's real though.

If you already have a loan or credit card, follow these tips and use them wisely. Now, if you have gotten yourself into a tough position with your credit there are a few things that can help. Some say to protect yourself from using your credit card, have it cancelled. I want to caution you against this because it lowers your length of credit history as well as the amount of credit available (unused) to you. Instead of cancelling, a better option is to cut it up. Once you pay it off, if you decide to use it again you can always re-order a new one.

I said all this assuming that you have an income as well as a bank account. If you are not yet working, do not use credit because you have no ability to pay it back. You may or may not have use for an account if you are not working, but if you are working, open up an account. Learn how to use your debit card, pin number, how to purchase in store and on-line. Do your research and go for a bank or credit union with minimal or no fees. I've also learned that it is a good idea to have accounts with two institutions. One as your local bank or credit union, which should have less or no fees and may have higher interest for savings, which equals growth in your accounts. Larger corporations tend to have more fees, but there are ways around them. These accounts are good because the banks are national and/or global, which gives you better access when you travel and are on the go.

Next, let's discuss bringing in income. If you are working and happy kudos to you! Keep it going and keep pressing onward and upward. Save and work hard. If you have been at a job over 6 months and have proven your work, don't be afraid to go for that promotion or ask for a raise. Statistics show that men are paid more and get more raises than women. We can't control everything, but we can ask for what we are worth. This tends to be an uncomfortable topic for females. It's time to break out of our comfort and that glass ceiling! You don't have to settle. The worse a person can say is no, so go for it!

If you are not working, but would like to be, keep applying. It is not easy and not always quick finding work. When I was a teen and in my early 20's it was so much easier and better. You could walk into a place, ask for an application, fill it out, attach your resume, ask to speak with the manager and possibly get an interview and job offer on the spot. It is not like that anymore. You are applying on a computer that is not getting to know you as a person, nor does it really know if you are a good fit or not. Keep pressing through. The right opportunity will come along. Just be patient with the process and prepare well for interviews. Practice introducing yourself and background, know your strengths and weakness, and let your true passion and personality shine through. Many times we get stiff and super professional because we are nervous. That is normal, but connection can help to get you in the door. If you do not get the position you must remember that the part was meant for someone else and your role is on the way. Once again, make sure you appear neat, clean, and you are on time if not early for your interviews.

Once you get into a job, make it a habit to begin saving some of your money. This can be for a car, house, vacation, and or a rainy day fund. Even if it is just $5-25 each check, it will add up over time. A good rule of thumb is to have a set amount placed into your savings account automatically each paycheck. That way you know it is being saved and it is not as accessible until you are ready to use it. If you really want to save even more or things are tight, set a budget and stick to it. A budget is an estimate of your total income and expenses, usually calculated per month. Once you deduct all of the major bills, you can then see how much you have left to save, spend, give, or invest. Once you look at your receipts and bills you can also see where you may be able to cut back and spend less. You also want to develop a rainy day or emergency fund for just in case purposes. Your goal should be to save at least 90 days worth of bills, with the ultimate goal of saving at least 1-2 years worth of living expenses. These funds can be used for car repairs, home upkeep, in case you are ever laid off or fired, as well as other unexpected necessities.

There are also many ways to bring in additional income. If you have a skill, and you do although you may need to discover it, you have a tool to bring in extra funds. Here are a few examples of what you may be good at: doing hair, painting, sewing, drawing, fixing things, putting things together, typing, coding, graphics, writing, and the list goes on. You don't have to turn it into a business; it can just be extra money, so no pressure. If you love it and are good at it, you do have the option to turn any hobby into a profitable business if you choose. After all we are in the *age of the Entrepreneur*. Everybody and their great Auntie want to own a business. While I appreciate the goals and motivation behind it, entrepreneurship is not easy, and not for everybody. Social media and the Internet has just made it super easy and too glamorous looking. It takes blood, sweat, fatigue, and a few tears to really succeed as an entrepreneur in any field. It may or may not be for you, you have to decide that for yourself.

Because it is so popular and there are so many options I have to bring up network marketing as a source of income. If you have a social media account chances are you have been exposed to one of these opportunities or a few. Network marketing is a business model that takes on distributors to use and sell their products and they take on distributors under them, which brings them in more income and bonuses, they repeat, and the pyramid keeps building. Some people say they make a really good living in network marketing, while others struggle. It is really up to your skill set, dedication, and how bad you really want it to work for you. I have tried a few and never became rich, but I realize that I was not passionate enough about any of them. You have to believe in anything you sell. Timing is also a huge element because if it is new and produces results, you have a better chance at succeeding than with a market overly saturated with too many distributors. If you love a product and swear by it, it may be worth the effort because people can feel when passion is real.

For me, my role is to inspire and empower girls and women in my own God-given way, so I will be selling products that uplift and empower. It makes sense and will work for me because it is true for me. Find what works for you. Try not to be desperate in your approach. There may come a time when you really need money and are willing to try anything. Before you move though, get on your knees and talk to God. Speak on what you need, being as specific as possible. Lay out your options and ideas, because prayer is a conversation, and ask for a strategy. Don't forget that prayer is a two-way conversation. Be still and wait a while. He will give you the strategy. It may take a while, but it will come. You will feel peace about the idea and decision you make if it's from your Director. Once you have confirmation, then it is time to put it into action. Some say fake it until you make it. I say faith it until you make it. Pray, believe, and get to work. I know this is my strategy.

Honestly, at first I didn't have all of the financing for this book, I Faithed it. I don't always feel capable, but I decided that I will Faith it. I've been through a lot and could have stopped knowing that I don't have the background, network, or connections, but I am determined, so I will keep Faithing it! What I learned most through all I've been through was about myself. I am still strong, resilient, creative, and a gift, even with scars. See, sometimes we forget who and whose we are. If you believe in God, you are the child of a King, which makes you a Princess. Princesses grow up to be Queens. You are royalty darling! The entire universe belongs to God and that is your inheritance. You just have to have faith enough to believe you can access it. What we truly believe, we draw to us. Most of all, I learned that I am full of faith and I've decided to turn every painful moment into purpose. You must do the same. Challenge yourself to face your fears. When we fall and make mistakes, let's get up with new knowledge from the lesson. It's elevation season, so separation and dedication are necessary. It's time to level up!

1. What is your dream and how will you finance it?

2. What skills could you use to gain additional income if needed?

3. What is your credit score?

4. How will you build, maintain, and improve your credit score starting now?

5. Do you need to have more faith? If yes, in what area? If no, why not?

Chapter 14
The Soundtrack

Chapter 14
The Soundtrack

This is not your typical soundtrack. In this chapter you will find lists of songs that make you smile and will keep you pushing. Whether you find them on Youtube, iTunes, or other music streams, you can search to find them. Some you may know very well and others may be new to you, but try them out! Because you see, it's very important to monitor what you listen to. The wrong song at the wrong time can cause anger, lead to bad decisions, and can have a negative influence. While the right song can encourage you, ignite you, help you get through tough times, and make you feel like you can accomplish anything. This is why music is placed so strategically in movies. It provokes emotion and makes the moment more impactful.

The only thing more powerful than music is what you say to yourself, so be sure to speak to yourself kindly. No matter what anyone else has said or says, you have the last say for your life. When you make mistakes or things do not go as planned and you have a negative thought about it, reaffirm yourself. When 'I'm so stupid comes to mind', tell yourself 'I am smart. Even smart people make mistakes.' If you think to yourself 'I should have done_____ or I should have said
_____.' And you are feeling self-critical, remind yourself that you did your best. And if you could have done better, great! We all can do better. That just means you are learning, so *practice* the skill being taught in the future. Don't expect yourself to get everything over night. Everything takes time, so be patient with you. In the past I would not have given this advice, but treat yourself better than you do anyone else. You matter that much. Forgive yourself, hug yourself, speak kind words out loud to yourself, try new things, and allow yourself to make mistakes. Do nice deeds for yourself and spend quality time with yourself. The kinder you are to yourself, the kinder you will be to others, so it's a win for everybody. Plus,

most will follow suit in being kind to you because you have set the stage and standard on how to treat you.

As you are preparing for your role and perfecting your skill set throughout life, remember your worth and value. Smile, praise your Creator, and sing happy songs daily. The soundtrack of our lives is crucial to what we believe about our lives and ourselves. He did not and will not bring you to it, without a plan to bring you through it. Just follow the script He gives you and you will get there. For those days you want to give up or you are going through grief, I know it's hard, but you are not alone, keep hope. Know that you are not alone. These songs here can sure be instrumental in getting you through.

For Hope & Inspiration

1. Intentional by Travis Greene
2. Trust In You by Anthony Brown & Group Therapy
3. I Got That by Anthony Brown & Group Therapy
4. I Made It by Fantasia ft. Tye Tribbett
5. Help by Erica Campbell ft. Lecrae
6. Well Done by Erica Campbell
7. Not Lucky, I'm Loved by Jonathan McReynolds
8. You Will Win Season by Jekalyn Carr
9. Bigger by Jekalyn Carr
10. W.A.Y.S by Jhene Aiko
11. 16 at War by Karina Pasian
12. Hang On ft. Kierra Sheard
13. Work It Out by Tye Tribbett
14. I Didn't Know My Own Strength by Whitney Houston
15. Won't He Do it by Koryn Hawthorne
16. Your Spirit by Tasha Cobbs Leonard ft. Kierra Leonard
17. Awesome Remix by Charles Jenkins ft. Jessica Reedy, Isacree, Da'Truth, & Canton Jones
18. Worry by Willie Moore Jr.
19. Better Way by Willie Moore ft. Bizzle
20. I Am Moana by Auli'I Cravalho

21. Still Standing by Monica
22. Without Me by Fantasia ft. Kelly Rowland & Missy Elliott
23. Until I Pass Out by Uncle Reese
24. Listen by Marvin Sapp
25. I'm Blessed by Charlie Wilson ft. T.I.

We already know who runs the world, right?!!! To keep the momentum and to remind you of your beauty, power, and excellence, listen to these:

Girl Power

1. Girl on Fire by Alicia Keys
2. Stronger by Kelly Clarkson
3. Can't Raise A Man by K. Michelle
4. Shining by Beyonce ft. Jay-Z
5. Sorry by Beyonce
6. Who Run the World by Beyonce
7. Survivor by Destiny's Child
8. Beautiful by Christina Aguilera
9. Fight Song by Rachel Platten
10. Love Myself by Haillee Steinfield
11. Go Get It by Mary Mary
12. God In Me by Mary Mary
13. Can't Bring Me Down by Karina Pasian
14. Roar by Katy Perry
15. Rise by Katy Perry
16. S.E.X. by Lyfe Jennings
17. Statistics by Lyfe Jennings
18. Bad Blood ft. Kendrick Lamar
19. Crzy ft Kehlani
20. Who Says by Selena Gomez
21. Who I Am by Jessica Andrews
22. Fly Above by Kandi Buruss
23. Shake You Off by Mariah Carey
24. My Life by The Walls Group
25. Like This by Kelly Rowland ft. Eve

These are all power songs and they are on my play list as well. I have praised and danced my way through stress, heartache, and pain. The cool thing about listening to this type of music is that it is for everybody. My 8-year-old and 3-year-old daughters know the words to each song, at least the choruses. I catch them singing them on their own all of the time and I join right in. What I love is that these songs plant seeds, so one day they will lean on and stand on these words as well. As the seeds are being planted in your own had and those around you, be sure to water them with love and kindness. Add some sunshine by stepping out on faith into all you are called to do. Then with patience, watch your mind and circumstances grow. It won't be easy and you will fall at least once (most likely more). Be sure of that. But you can also be sure that you will get back up stronger, wiser, and bolder than before.

It was tough keeping these lists to 25 because there are so many great songs, Artists, Producers, and beat makers that make magic. They are in no particular order, these are the songs that came to the forefront and were played on repeat during the timeframe I was writing, editing, and promoting this book. Feel free to add, subtract, listen to, and replay these songs when you need a boost. Thank you to all of the Writers, Artists, Producers, Directors, and others who helped these songs come to life for the world! These songs uplift, empower, and may be saving lives. With all of this said, pause, breathe, cry, press play, dance, pray, cry some more, laugh, plan, implement, and keep going! Keep believing in your greatness! To God be the glory!

1. What are the 3 top songs on your daily playlist right now? How do these songs make you feel?

2. List two songs from the list above that you have never heard until now, which uplift you? Write about how and any why?

3. Check out Our Deepest Fear by Marianne Williamson. I love this poem! It has helped to inspire my title for this book and it inspires me. I first heard a peace of it in the movie Coach Carter. It brought me to tears of joy with its power. It is pretty deep and an attack of the enemy putting fear in its place. Ever since I've heard it, I've been sharing it and living it more every day. Does this poem strike a chord with you? If yes, how and what lines reach you? What do they mean to you?

4. What is something negative you have caught yourself saying or thinking to yourself about yourself? Write it down. Now, write the opposite of it on another sheet of paper. Throw out the paper with the negativity. Speak the positive opposite thing or idea over yourself right now and daily. For example, If you have ever said "I'm so stupid" write that down. On another sheet of paper write "I am very intelligent". Throw out that stupidity paper and tell yourself how smart and intelligent you are "I am so smart." Do this 2-3 times each day. This is called an affirmation. Affirm great things over yourself. It's time to break the chain!

5. What are 5-7 great characteristics about yourself? Yes your gorgeous, but no more than 2 should include looks.

Chapter 15
The Premiere

Ch. 15
The Premiere

You Ready!?! The carpet is laid out. The lights are placed just right and people are watching. Fans, supporters, family, friends, bystanders, and even folks who want you to fail, they are all watching. Say to yourself, *I Am Enough* and let's give them a show! The carpet is purple to represent royalty because darling that's what you are. The red carpet is a bit common, don't you think? And you are far from common. You are special and unique- never forget that. Just be you and people who are meant for you will love and accept you as you are or they will guide you. Don't hide from your difference. Your difference is what sets you apart and will get you to the places you are trying to go. As you plot your coming out and being all of you party, be sure to bring it! Showing up is looking fly and acting as you please, but it's also more than that. Be sure to show up with your lessons and wisdom. When you encounter pain, be sure to turn that thing into purpose. This purpose can impact and help others. Even if it's only one person you help, that's enough. Just being you in all of your light can help other people to accept and love themselves, so shine brightly.

As I am writing this book I am in awe of the script that my Higher Power has written for me. Just days ago I learned that I was nominated and chosen to be honored at the 100 Women of Color Gala for 2018. What an honor it is! I was in shock when I read it. That's bananas! See this gala has been going on for some years and it's all about empowering women. For years I've wanted to go, but I haven't been able to attend due to financial constraints. I was finally going to be able to get my ticket this year so that I could be in the audience and cheer on my beautiful sisters who are doing so much in our communities. But my God! He had other plans. He saw fit that I would not just be a spectator, but I would walk across that stage and receive an award. What?!!! Amazing! Did I see this coming? Yes and no. I say yes because yes, this was a dream of mine. I know how much I plan to do for my community and I thought that one day I'd be recognized for it. The answer for right now though is no, because I had hoped to receive this award about 2-3 years from now. That was my goal. But look at God. He said with all of the sacrifice, empowering others, and stepping out on faith to be a light, "you will be honored now".

So tell me why I had to read it twice and for a moment I felt like there was some mistake. I mean, this gala honors 100 women from Southern CT all the way up through Northern MA. That's a lot of women to choose from! I'm on social media and there are plenty of women doing great work to help our schools, communities, hospitals, and more. Listen, Anika Noni Rose and Regina King are being honored there this year *right beside me*! Super bananas! I would be lying if I said that I don't still have moments when I feel undeserving. I have been on planning committees and have volunteered for events lead by other women, but I have not held my own yet. I even asked God why, feeling as though I needed to be more accomplished before I received this award. Once I sat with it and sat with Him, I was able to see more clearly that I deserve every piece of this award. I was reminded of a few things. I have started an inspirational greeting card and apparel line to uplift girls and women. I became a #1 Best Selling Author last year of a great collaborative book. Daily and weekly I inspire and uplift women on social media and sometimes in person. I even get messages and comments from women seeking help and telling me that I am helping them. That is beautiful. I am not a therapist, but I am reaching people. *I had to remember that I Am Enough.* The key was to stop comparing and start being grateful for what I have been able to do.

He gifted me to help others and be a light and I had just been trying to dim it being afraid to stand out. He has shown you favor and grace as well, you just have to look for it, accept it, and maybe change your perspective. It's sometimes easier to focus on negativity, but we're changing this. Right? When God chooses you, He chooses you, and you may not always know why. And for me, this goes way back. I mean back to elementary school. I remember being in 6th grade and receiving the Martin Luther King Kid Award. The student body voted on this award and I was not counting on it. Lord knows I was shocked and happy, but I did not know why. I knew that I was a great, smart, and a kind person, but didn't know how others viewed me nor understood what I did to deserve it. This is another reminder that others see things in us that we don't always see in ourselves. It's usually a good thing unless there is jealousy and ulterior motives. This was easy for me when I was young, but as I grew older I wanted to impress as well as to fit in. I never did anything crazy to do so, but I just wanted to be accepted. Then I was showed I was accepted and maybe admired. It was pretty cool and a bit scary. I was responsible at an early age. We aren't always told this, but this is a desire of all human beings. We all want to be accepted. So there is no need to hide any parts of you, personality wise. It won't always be friends, family, or whom you thought, but the right folks do and will accept you. You Are Enough!

And for the record, let me say this: It is okay to adjust yourself in public. No, you do not want your assets out, so be appropriate, but it just fine to fix your clothing or hair outside of the bathroom. Growing up I always heard "ladies don't adjust themselves in public" so this left me with a strong thought that I could only fix my hair, clothes, and makeup in my bedroom, at home, or in a restroom. Of course, you don't want your tighten your bra, pull your pants down, or skirt up at a dinner table (or in any public space) but it is ok to straighten your shirt, tuck in your shirt, and twist your pant leg right in public. These things should offend no one and if it does, that's not your problem. For sure you want to do the bulk of your prep n private, but things move and sometimes we rush. So it is ok to check yourself out. Look at yourself from your clothes to your toes and adjust anything you feel you need to, to your liking. I learned this after attending events and later looking at pictures and wishing I would've checked and altered a few things, like adjusting my shirt, centering my pants, pushed my hair back, etc. Then I've watched models and celebrities and they or their stylist adjust their hair and clothing all the time. If you have been taught that 'ladies don't adjust themselves' or anything else, do your own research then do what's comfortable for you. I like great pictures and memories so I have to do what works for me. Work toward always being in the moment and getting your vision captured without thinking about your surroundings.

I grew up in the inner city and my family members all had humble beginnings, so at some point I stopped shining intentionally. I am an introvert by nature, so I'm quiet, but I chose to be silent about my accomplishments and never boasted like some people. I didn't want anyone thinking, "Who does she think she is?" I was afraid that family and friends would be jealous or put me on some up pedestal for my good grades, awards, new jobs, and fun parties, so I censored myself when sharing. I didn't even share with enthusiasm many times when I did talk. I wanted folks to think, *It's not that big of a deal.* I can't tell you where I got this from other than fear. I did not have many examples of excitement, succeeding, and acceptance. So I pretended to be a mediocre individual living as those I knew. The crazy thing about this is that still, I fell, got bruised, and needed help a couple of times and people still talked badly. People will always have something to say, so do you, be you, and please you unapologetically.

Now, if you are surrounded by support and it's just you in your own way putting limits on yourself, then it's a little different. This is me at times as well, so I understand. Sometimes we are our worst critics and belittle our accomplishments because we are not yet where we want to be. The key word is, yet. You will get there. You are not there yet, but respect the journey. It takes practice and patience to reach goals. Any expert, specialist, or champion, was once a beginner. It is time to break free of the self-critical habit. Everyone you see as successful had and has a journey that's not always easy. If you have a vision and are on your way there, enjoy the journey, and be ok with getting celebrated all the way to the destination.

I decided that I'm showing up to my life premiere fully decorated in classiness. Class is just my way of doing things, hence the name Classy Chrisy. I believe in being tactful in my approach, communication and style. Yours may be different, but we all can carry something classic. Class is missing nowadays and it needs to make a full comeback. Our girls don't have enough classy images to copy. I want to be that. If you are or want to be a leader, let's give them that! Why not us?! It seems that the less clothes some where on the carpet and other wise, the more attention they receive. As some say, I guess *sex sells*. Well what about class? When I see a girl or woman turning heads with her assets covered and dressed appropriately, to me, she is Queen. When you can do that, you know you are hot. Maybe this role isn't for everyone, but it is for you if you want it. You are meant to lead in class in your own way. So what I'll say about class is *Class is expensive, not all can afford it,* spread the word! Now run to tell that. Not everyone can handle or afford to be classy. And I don't mean spend a lot, just be a lady and dress accordingly. Can you rock that price tag of tasteful, yet expensive class? I think you can. #ClassIsExpensive

Your past doesn't matter. This book is geared toward teenagers and 20-something year olds, but it doesn't matter how young or old or young you are, it's not too early or too late for you. You lack nothing, you may not even realize it, but you have more than what it takes. So take the steps of faith where you can and the Director will fill in the blanks where you are unable. Lack is just a state of mind, that's why we need to be sure to stay connected to positivity. Our minds hold power and feed off of energy and information, both negative and positive. I choose positivity. You may not have the best influences in your family or nearby, but you can still get you a mentor or a few. We all could use a few mentors being spiritual, financial, fitness, purpose, and business. Mentors do cost money because it is their time and they have to make a living too. You may find all you need in one mentor or find that you need more than one mentor. Choose whatever works best for you. If you just don't have the finances, another option is to reach out to a woman doing what you plan to do someday. Ask her how you can be of assistance to her mission. You will be surprised as to who will say yes, please, and thank you to your offer. By her side you will get real world experience, learn the ins and outs, gain contacts, and gain a great reference. Don't get offended if anyone says no, that means it's not for you at this time. There are plenty of other possible mentors, so keep searching. Find a way to get things done when there is a call on your life with or without the means. Someone is waiting on you to show up and they can literally miss out on what they need if you don't push forward because your example and your story are the answer. No pressure. You got this!

Oprah spoke on stage to a graduating class and she said, "I am full of myself!" I thought that this was so powerful. She like me, used to be afraid of being seen as being *full of myself* or overly confident. If not you, who else will you be full of? My advice is for you to stay connected to the source so that you can be full until you are over flowing, so that you can pour out into others.

You may have moments when you are afraid to show your true self. That stage of life with all of the attention seems fun, but it can be scary. This is a great time to remind yourself, '*I Am Enough!*' There's no need to worry because in your weakness, God can show His strength. If you begin to do the work, He will exalt and promote you when you least expect it. To make an impact, one has to be bold. You have to walk with confidence, talk like you belong in the room, and believe that you can do all things you set out to do. No one talks, thinks, walks, or has the exact vision as you do, so carry out that thing! The goal is to be happy when you look into the mirror. You were created to make huge impact! So who are you not to write that book? Not to star in that movie? Not to be a Teacher? Who are you Not to be a Law Maker or an Influencer? Not to go to school to prepare to be a surgeon? Who are you not to fill this world with all of the greatness put inside of you? You must! He created you and is preparing you for that purpose. Ask yourself "Who Am I? What do I deserve? How can I make it happen? Am I limitless?" The answer to those last two questions is YES baby girl! If you have Faith and consider yourself one of God's children, then who are you not to shine?" You were chosen for the main character role in the movie of the century! This is the most important role of your life. Congratulations!!! Enjoy it and live it boldly! As you shine, you will light the way for others.

And remember, always do your best and expect the best, because you deserve the best. It's time to shine!

1. Have you ever battled with hiding your greatness?

2. Are you afraid to be all of you? If yes, in what settings and what are you going to do about this?

3. What are you most excited about regarding showing up in your own life?

4. Do you have any mentors? Will you be getting any (more) mentors? If yes which ones? If no, why not?

5. Are you doing your best in all you do? If yes, how do you know? If not, what changes are you about to make?

P.S.

Now that you are discovering who you are and why you are here, be sure to remember this every time you have a decision to make. Don't let people who are off track get you sidetracked. Continue to unwrap every experience good or bad and you will reveal more of your purpose. The life you dream may seem far away, but if you believe it, you can create it- maybe sooner than you think. If you are truly ready to take the lead, ready to perform, and you know your Director has your back, get ready to shine! And, if you must shine on that stage, and you must, do it with class!

Love,

Classy Chrisy

About the Author

Christina Johnson is an Educator, Writer and an Image Advocate that is all about spreading positivity, empowerment, and encouragement. As a #1 Best Selling Author of the book collaboration *30/30 Rules: What I Wish I Knew in My 20's,* Christina is also a 100 Women of Color, Class of 2018 Honoree. She promotes sisterhood, love, respect for self and others. She created Shine, a multi-cultural greeting card, apparel, and accessory line to uplift girls and women. Christina is a contributing writer for Just Be U Magazine; she loves fashion, but is not a fan of trends. She believes in respecting and accepting differences as key points in purpose. Christina holds a BA in Mass Media Communication, from the University of Hartford and an MFA in Media Design from Full Sail University. With a desire to serve, Christina has just begun. When she is not working or writing Christina enjoys painting, dancing, reading, yoga, relaxing at the beach, and spending time with her husband and two amazing daughters. Christina's greatest mission is to inspire others in finding and strengthening their value in self-awareness, self-love, class, and walking toward purpose. Connect with me @ClassyChrisy on Facebook, Instagram, and Twitter.

Be sure to add and watch for the tags:
#WhoAmINotToShine?
#PurposeOverPerfect
#FaithOnFleek
#ClassIsNeverOutofStyle
#FullyDressedAndKillingIt